The Family Book Of
BOATING

By MIKE KAPLAN

GALAHAD BOOKS · NEW YORK CITY

PHOTO CREDITS

Aluma Craft Page 138
American National Red Cross
    Page 159
Amphicar Page 141
Bonair Boats, Inc. Page 140
Century Pages 25, 30
Chrysler Pages 70, 126, 128, 135
Du Pont Page 113
Evinrude Pages 4, 26, 115, 118
Glastron Page 60
Grover Page 48
Johnson & Johnson Page 156
Johnson Motors Pages 8 & 9,
    150, 152
Kenner Manufacturing Co., Inc.
    Page 131
Kiekhaefer Mercury Page 80

Lehman Manufacturing Co., Inc.
    Page 47
Michigan Wheel Company Page 66
Mobil Oil Corporation Pages 75, 76,
    79, 99
Pacemaker Pages 4 & 5, 14 & 15, 56,
    73
Penn Yan Pages 36, 32
Perkins Engines Page 29
Striker Pages 12, 121
Trojan Boat Company,
    Pages 23, 34, 63
U.S. Department of Commerce,
    Weather Bureau Pages 104, 105,
    106, 107
U.S. Navy Training Publications
    Center Pages 88 & 89

Copyright © 1973 by Stadia Sports Publishing, Inc., 180 Madison Avenue,
New York, N.Y.

Library of Congress Catalog Card Number: 74-78144
ISBN: 0-88365-292-7

Published by arrangement with Stadia Sports Publishing, Inc.

Manufactured in the United States of America

TABLE OF CONTENTS

CHAPTER ONE

The Power Boat

Well over fifty million enthusiasts enjoy the exhilarating sport of boating.

■ Recent years have witnessed a tremendous growth in the sport of boating. Going out onto the open waters has rapidly become one of the favorite ways of spending leisure time for an ever-increasing number of people. This is particularly true as regards the family-group which seeks an activity or pastime in which all its members can become involved and be participants rather than mere spectators. It has been reliably estimated that there are well over fifty million people who spend at least a part of their leisure time enjoying the infinite fun of riding over the waters in a boat.

There are a number of factors which have contributed to this sport's rise in popularity lately. One major reason for the public's increase in boating participation has been the development of the highly-efficient and relatively simple-to-operate outboard motor. Another contributing factor has been the almost limitless variety of available hull designs. There are a fantastic number of combinations of hull designs and motors from which to choose. This makes it possible for anyone to purchase a vessel which is perfectly suited to meet the exact requirements of the boatman and his family-group. Also, because of the possibility of choosing a combination of hull design and motor which is tailored to meet each individual's own need and taste, there are boats that can be had which are within the financial reach of just about everybody who has a real, deep desire to own his personal power craft. Another very important reason for the great rise in boating's popularity, especially in the field of power boats, is that the skills necessary for the efficient operation of one of these joy-giving rigs are easily learned after only a short period of instruction.

Motor powered boats account for over three-quarters of the sales of all boats ... and well over two-thirds of all power boats purchased are of the outboard vari-

Motorboats are overwhelmingly popular.

ety. There are many different types of powered boats being purchased by eager-to-be boat owners, each type having its own personality and its own operating characteristics. On the following pages, we shall discuss some of these different types in detail.

RUNABOUTS

If there is any one boat which can be said to have been designed specifically for fun and speed, that one boat would most certainly have to be the runabout. The description fits this craft perfectly. Runabouts are open, family-type sport boats. Most of them range from fourteen to twenty feet in length. Their open design allow for easy boarding and leaving as well as easy freedom of movement for those on board. Runabouts are known for their speed and high degree of maneuverability. Most of them are powered by outboard motors which are in the 35 to 75 hp range. A great percentage of them have their hulls constructed of either fiberglass or plywood.

Of all the vast numbers of available hull designs, two particular designs have come to be used almost exclusively for runabouts. One of these hull designs is shown as a tri-hull and the other is designated the V-hull. Because of its greater width at the bow, many boatmen consider the tri-hull the more stylish of the two designs. But this is only one of the reasons for its greater popularity with family-group boat purchasers. The greater bow-width makes forward seating possible and gives adults more opportunity to keep closer vigil on any youngsters who may be on board. Another considerable advantage of the tri-hull design is its ability to cross heavy seas.

The V-hull is a more specialized type of runabout. The design of the V-hull allows it to present a relatively small surface area to the water through which it is skimming. This helps to reduce friction and enables the V-hull to get faster starts and aids it to handle better than a tri-hull of comparable size. Because of its advantage of accelerating faster and handling easier, the V-hull runabout is very

often used as the pulling vehicle for water-skiers. It's high degree of maneuverability makes this hull design ideal for the sport of water skiing. More often than not, the V-hulls which are used for this purpose are equipped with outboard motors of at least 60 hp. Also, because of its minimal amount of friction, or drag in the water, V-hulls are commonly used in boat racing.

While runabouts are good-looking, sleek, fast, and highly maneuverable, there is something they are not. They are not at all suitable for long-distance cruising nor are they the proper boats to use in heavy seas. They have neither the size, stability, or capacity for such use.

HYDROPLANES

Hydroplanes are among the most specialized of all sports boats. Their hulls are designed for one purpose and one purpose only . . . SPEED. These speed boats are made specifically for racing and just plain fast travel. They are most often occupied by just one boatman, although there are sometimes two speed-demons occupying a hydroplane.

The hydroplane actually derives its name from its ability to skim or "plane" the surface of the water. The hull is so designed that when one of these speedsters is really moving, there is only a bare minimum of the hull area which is in actual contact with the water. It is almost literally flying over the water. When speed is either desired or needed, the hydroplane is no doubt the epitome of marine transportation devices. A great

The hydroplane was designed for one purpose only . . . speed over the water!

deal of care and attention is paid to combining the hull design with the proper power plant. These highly specialized sport boats have their hulls fitted with power plants that are ideally suited to each other so that they can "plane" with the greatest of ease. By using a well-designed and proper hull area, it is extraordinarily easy to achieve speeds of 16 Miles Per Hour with no more than a 7.5 hp motor. That is how highly efficient the hydroplane hull is in achieving speed. With no more than a 25 hp motor, it is quite possible to achieve speeds of 30 mph.

More speed records on water have been gained by hydroplanes than by any other types of hull design. There is no doubt but that one of the most exhilarating and exciting rides a person can experience is a flat-out trip in a high-powered hydroplane.

UTILITY BOATS

These are the least expensive boats in a builder's line. They are more or less stripped-down versions of the runabouts. The hull of a utility boat is very often identical to that of a runabout. Therefore, it can be powered sufficiently so that it too can give the same speed as its more sleek and expensive sister model. Of course, the utility boat will provide far less comfort along with its reduced trim. But, when economy is of prime interest and you have a deep, abiding desire to own a small, all-around boat, the utility boat is your answer. Of course, this rig will afford you the opportunity to add equipment as your financial ability permits and your heart desires. With money and desire, the "ugly duckling" utility boat can easily be converted to a "Swan" of a runabout.

Very often, utility boats are referred to as fishing boats. This may be a very apt description of them as most utility boats are used for the prime purpose of getting one or two fishermen out to where the fish are waiting. After all, there is no more flexible fish finder than a small boat outfitted with an outboard motor. It sure makes the going much easier and pleasant and quicker than rowing or paddling. And after a long day out in the fresh air, under a bright, warm sun, the powered utility boat makes the going home that much easier. Most of the utility boats used for this purpose are of the row-boat type, having a hull design much like a flat-bottomed skiff. These range from ten to sixteen feet in length and are generally made of fiberglass, plywood, or wood planking. While they resemble the standard rowboat, they are somewhat modified to accommodate an outboard motor.

Another type of utility boat is the one referred to earlier . . . the one which has a hull design identical to the runabouts. These vary in size from twelve to twenty-four feet in length and are designed to get the most speed and power from available outboard motors. These are planing-hull boats which have either round or V-bottoms. Their large beams make them very stable and they can take outboard motors of anywhere from 7.5 hp

up to 75 hp, depending on the hull size. The larger the boat, the higher the hp needed. Adequately powered utility boats can be just as fast as runabouts and it is not at all uncommon to see a utility boat being used for pulling people on water skis.

HOUSEBOATS

A very specialized type of powered boat is the houseboat. While it is an offshoot of a cruiser or, if large enough, a motor yacht, the houseboat is specifically designed to allow its owners and guests more permanent-type living while on board and also for operating in better protected, shallower waters than the standard cruiser or motor yacht. The houseboat is definitely not manufactured for use in coastal or open waters . . . and it should never be taken out into these areas. Instead, because of its provisions for living comforts, the houseboat has known a steadily-increasing growth in popularity as a means for travelling along lakes, rivers, and other inland waterways.

Because its prime concern lies with providing its passengers with living conditions closely resembling those they would enjoy at home, the houseboat probably offers more usable space per dollar of cost than any other type of boat on the market. A common houseboat layout will comprise a well-equipped galley (kitchen) wherein the person who is doing the cooking for those aboard can practise all his or her culinary talents as they would do at home. This is usually located directly amidship (center section) where

The houseboat is manufactured to provide shore-style living while afloat.

tranquil and fairly shallow inland waters, can be made of either aluminum or plywood, thereby avoiding the extra expense of using the special, more sturdy materials used in the construction of open-sea vessels. Another factor contributing to the rather inexpensive furnishing of a houseboat is its size of living quarters. This makes it possible to avoid the use of costly compact appliances and instead, make use of less expensive, standard equipment such as stoves and refrigerators.

The moving power of a houseboat can be derived from either inboard or outboard motors. Even the largest of these floating homes-away-from-home can be powered sufficiently so that it can move along at speeds exceeding thirty miles-per-hour.

THE SPORTFISHERMAN

This is just about the most specialized of all the powered boats in use today. The sportfisherman and the cruiser have power plants which are similar and they are also alike in size. However, there the similarity ends.

While technically speaking, the term "sportfisherman" can be applied to just about any boat, from utility to cruiser, a recent trend has been to restrict the term to those boats which have cruising capabilities and are more than thirty feet in length. Therefore, for the purpose of distinguishing the sportfisherman from the other powered boats, we will only be concerned with those boats which are longer than thirty feet and

any rocking or seesawing motion is kept to minimal noticeability. There is also usually a dinette which converts to a bedroom sleeping two, a living room also convertible to sleeping quarters, and ample head (lavatory) facilities. Of course, provisions are made for supplying hot and cold running water, shower rooms, front and back porches which can be enclosed if so desired, and a sundeck. Houseboats range anywhere from eighteen to more than forty feet in length. Even the smallest of these has sufficient room so that it can sleep four in comfort.

One of the prime factors in the simplification of the construction of modern houseboats and in the lowering of the costs of building them has been the development of the planing hull. This has made it possible to eliminate the use of compound curves and jutting frame members which only served to complicate the construction of a houseboat and tended to take space away from the living quarters. Also, houseboats being designed for travelling in usually

Perhaps the most highly specialized power boat today is the sportfisherman.

have cruising capabilities and are outfitted to perform the prime function of pursuing and landing big-game fish. To help it meet the obligation of its purpose, the sportfisherman has most of its usable space devoted to the sport of catching and landing fish. The builders of these types of boats are not at all concerned with large, plush cabin areas or extravagantly decorated interiors. Instead, the interiors of a sportfisherman are most often sparsely outfitted, consisting of a small galley, a functional but not luxurious head, and a bare minimal dinette. The cockpit is generally quite large, thereby reducing the area devoted to cabin space. The sportfisherman is easily recognized by many of its distinguishing construction features. It has a much lower freeboard than a cruiser, which puts the big-game angler much closer to the water. This makes it easier for him to fight his catch and also facilitates the landing of a good-sized fish. Part of the deck area at the stern of a sportfisherman is utilized as a fish well wherein the catch is held. A sportfisherman is also equipped with a flying bridge from which the skipper steers and otherwise controls the boat. This flying bridge is located above the cabin. By locating the control station high above the deck, the skipper has a much better view of the water surrounding the boat and is in a better position to locate the sought-for fish. The large cockpit area is equipped with at least one fighting chair which is a specially-

designed seat for the angler; there is a gin pole, or hoist, which is used to boat really large catches; a storage room in which the tackle necessary for big-game fishing is kept until needed; a tuna tower is a fairly standard piece of equipment for a sportfisherman, as are outriggers, fish finders, gaffs, and other paraphernelia specifically designed to catch big fish.

CRUISERS

Those powered boats that fall into the cruiser category are split into two distinct classes: the cabin cruiser and the day cruiser. Most cruisers are powered by outboard motors and are capable of wending their way through the open seas. Also, all cruisers are equipped with an enclosed cabin as well as a cockpit area. It is in the area of prime purpose and design that the day cruiser and the cabin cruiser have their differences.

The cabin cruiser is the more luxurious of the two, having as its prime purpose the transporting of passengers who are on a vacation and want to spend that vacation comfortably riding over the seas. This floating vacation spot features a fully-enclosed cabin area and will vary in length from sixteen to twenty-five feet. For the average family, a twenty-two-footer is considered by knowledgeable boatmen to be optimum size. There is a "Sedan" class of cabin cruiser which has a minimum of six feet of headroom through its cabin area. This extra-large, luxurious cabin is attained by constructing a smaller than standard cockpit area. In view of the fact that the cabin cruiser is to

One of the more elegant boats plying the waters is known as the cabin cruiser.
Here is a truly luxurious, floating, home-away-from home.

be used for relatively long periods of time (anywhere from a weekend to several weeks), it comes equipped with adequate fuel and fresh water facilities as well as comfortable sleeping, lavatory, and shower facilities, which make it quite comfortable.

The day cruiser is actually a toned-down modification of the cabin cruiser. Its prime purpose being a means of its owner and passengers going fishing rather than vacationing with extended living aboard, the day cruiser is constructed on a far less luxurious scale and is accordingly far less costly. In view of the fact that day cruisers are mostly utilized as fishing vessels, they have larger cockpit areas and correspondingly smaller cabin areas. Builders of day cruisers modify the true cruiser by skimping on or completely eliminating one or more of the luxury features. The hardest hit feature is that area devoted to sleeping facilities. After all, adequate fuel and fresh water supplies as well as lavoratory facilities and a galley are as necessary when out for a day of fishing as they are when out for several days of voyaging. Of course, the galley, or kitchen, area does not have to be as extensive nor as well appointed as it would be on a cruiser because the time spent on board will be of relatively short duration. Day cruisers range from fifteen to twenty-two feet in length and are sometimes referred to as "weekenders." This indicates that there are some hardy souls that could probably endure a night or even two, if necessary, aboard one of these craft.

MOTOR YACHTS

When we start talking about motor yachts, we are entering the realm of absolute luxury, leisure, and comfort within the world of powered boats. Comparing a utility boat or a runabout to a motor yacht is tantamount to comparing a moderately-priced ranch house to a luxurious mansion. Much the same as mansions, motor yachts come in many different forms and designs. But also like mansions, they all have several common features. Motor yachts don't generally come any smaller than fifty feet in length, with many of them being considerably longer. All of them are equipped with large tanks capable of taking on considerable quantities of fuel and fresh water. This makes it psosible for these floating estates to make lengthy cruises far off into the open seas. Each of the lounging and operating departments of a yacht, such as the galley area and the navigating control stations, is located with just about every conceivable accessory item money can buy ... especially those that fall into the electronic class.

The average motor yacht's layout will generally consist of two or more luxuriously-appointed staterooms, a comfortable and well-equipped lounging salon, a less-lavish cabin for at least one hired hand (which is traditionally located in the forward part of the yacht, as the owner's and guest staterooms are located in the stern), and a deckhouse wherein is located the steering or helmsman station. A motor yacht is also generally equipped with a generator which is capable of producing

The ultimate step upward for the would-be skipper is into the heady atmosphere occupied by the most lavish of all pleasure craft, the motor yacht.

Truly luxurious interior appointments are the hallmark of the motor yacht.

This majestic yacht heads seaward, well-equipped for a lengthy cruise.

enough electricity to run all its electronic accessories as though the yacht was tied up to a dock on shore.

The power plant of a motor yacht generally consists of two separate engines, each engine driving its own propeller. The really large yachts usually have their engines driven by diesel power. Most of the hulls for motor yachts are constructed of wood.

HYDROFOILS

Alexander Graham Bell, who is far more noted and reknowned as the inventor of the telephone, was the first person to experiment with the hydrofoil in this country. So one can readily see that this is no johnny-come-lately form of water transportation. However, this type of craft has as yet not become overwhelmingly popular. Yet, it has some highly desirable qualitites.

A hydrofoil has an extremely efficient planing hull which has two thin foils affixed to it, one foil on each side. When the boat is powered sufficiently to attain planing speed, the hull is literally lifted completely out of the water and only the foil sides rest on the surface of the water. In view of the fact that the hull is riding a number of feet above the water line, it can readily be seen that the passengers in one of these craft would experience an extremely dry ride. There is no chance of water coming into the boat over the sides and there is almost a total lack of spray. In addition to this endearing quality, only the

relatively small surface of the foil members is subject to the rolling motion of the waves. This enables the hydrofoil to ride through even rather rough water quite smoothly.

Fairly recently, hydrofoils have been experimentally used as commuter boats in the harbor of New York City. We will be watching these experiments with a great deal of interest. Wouldn't it be something if hydrofoils were to replace, at least in part, the Long Island Railroad as a means of many Long Islanders commuting from their homes to their places of business in the Big Town?

MOTOR SAILERS

In theory, the motor sailer is a hybrid offshoot of the motorboat

Motor sailer, the best of both worlds.

and the sailboat. Theoretically, this craft is supposed to be one half of the former and one half of the latter. However, in actuality, it doesn't work out quite that way. Most models of this craft are custom built rather than mass-produced as stock items in a boatbuilders line of boats. Therefore, most motor sailers wind up leaning toward one of the other means of forward propulsion; either they are predominantly motorboat and only incidentally sailboat, or they are predominantly sailboat and only incidentally motorboat.

When the motor sailer is designed primarily as a motorboat, the sail is unfurled and hoisted merely to conserve the fuel supply and, possibly, to help keep the boat on a more steady course when the wind starts to come up somewhat briskly. On the other hand, when the primary design of the boat is as a sailboat, the motor is used to help steady a course while riding before a wind or, more importantly, to continue on course in the absence of propelling wind. The motor can also be of great assistance when negotiating a heavily-trafficked anchorage or getting into a tricky marina slip.

AUXILIARY

These relatively small boats are basically sailboats. However, they are distinguished from the usual run of sailboats by the fact that they are equipped with an outboard motor, usually of rather small horsepower. The motor is meant to provide only enough power to serve as an auxiliary source of propulsion to the sail in

the event such additional power should be necessary because of a loss of wind or to aid when berthing the vessel. Of course, when the auxiliary is being moved under power, it is considered a motorboat. As such, it is subject to all the same rules of behavior as any other motor powered water craft.

DO-IT-YOURSELF BOATS

There are kits which can be purchased from almost all of the leading boatbuilding firms with which the "do-it-yourselfer" can build his own boat. These kits come with complete easy-to-follow, step-by-step sets of instructions.

There are several ways in which these plans can be used. The ambitious do-it-yourselfer can just buy the plans from the boatbuilder and then purchase the necessary building materials from a local supplier. The plans themselves usually cost only a few dollars. Or, if he prefers, the amateur boatbuilder can buy just the hull and put everything else together himself. Another option is to purchase a complete kit from a boatbuilding firm. A kit of this kind can be assembled with no more than ordinary hand tools, providing you can read the plans.

In view of the fact that the most expensive part going into a new boat is the labor that it took to build it, it is possible to build a boat yourself at a saving of anywhere from fifty to sixty-five percent. Depending on the complexity of the boat, a complete kit can be assembled in a period of about six weeks. That is, by working nights and weekends. ●

CHAPTER TWO

Boat Terminology

■ Each and every year, an ever-increasing number of Americans are purchasing their first boats. And with their purchase, they quickly start to experience that very special, wonderful feeling of freedom that boat ownership and possession imparts. However, all too many of these new "captains" fail to realize that there is more to boating than the simple act of buying a boat. There is a long and colorful history to boating ... and boating has a tradition all its very own. And a large part of that tradition is boating's special language. While it is true that technological advancement has had a great deal of effect on the face of boating over the past several decades, the language, or terminology, has for the most part remained unchanged. Much as the learning of a country's language helps the student to also learn a good deal of that particular country's past history, so is the learning the language of boating a means of making contact with and becoming a part of that pastime's colorful past.

There is, even more importantly, a practical reason for studying and learning the language of boats and boating. Boat terminology is quite concise and is a definite means of communication and instant understanding. As an example of this, let us assume that you and your family have been out for an enjoyable day of cruising around in your new "toy." Now you are back in port and are in the act of mooring your vessel. Suddenly, your lovely and helpful wife (she's probably been designated first-mate in the crew) shouts, "Look out for the left side!" Should she happen to be facing in the opposite direction than you, it is quite likely that your new boat will make shocking and possibly damaging contact with the dock. However, were she to yell, "Look out to port!" and you were likewise familiar with proper boat terminology, you would instantly know what she meant. Port, in boat language, always means the left side of the boat in relation to the front of the boat (which, incidentally, is always called the bow). So, in the example cited, if you were facing the front of the boat, you would know she meant the left side; if you were facing the back of the boat (always called the stern), it would still mean the left side of the boat except that now it would be to your right. See what we mean?

The following simplified boat diagram and the accompanying glossary of standard boat and boating terms will not automatically turn you into an experienced, veteran boatman. This is not its intent. But the combination will provide you with a basis for better understanding your boat and the boats you will find around you when you sail out. This understanding and greater ability to communicate with others in and out of the water will surely increase the enjoyment you and your family will derive from owning a boat.

GLOSSARY OF TERMS:

Abeam: alongside, abreast of the boat

Aft: at or near the rear of the boat

Amidships: middle of the boat; halfway between the front and the rear

Astern: behind the boat

Athwartships: from side to side of the boat; opposite of fore-and-aft

Bail: to throw water from a boat

Barnacle: form of salt-water marine life which grows on ship bottoms

Beam: greatest width of a boat

Below: under the deck

Berth: mooring place for a boat

Bilge: bottom of the hull

Bilge pump: a device to pump water from the hull

Binnacle: compass cover

Block: pully

Boat hook: a pole with a metal hook; used for retrieving objects from the water or for handling small boats alongside the dock

Ballards: short heavy beams on a pier, used for tying up boats

Boot top: thin strip of paint at the water line

Bow: front end of the boat

Bulkhead: boat wall

Car-topper: boat able to be carried atop a car

Cat-walk: deck alongside cabin

Cavitation: occurs when air is pulled from the surface to around the propeller; causes loss of power

Ceiling: lining of thin planks inside the rib

Chart: marine road map

Chine: lowest edge of the hull where sides and bottom join

Chock: horizontal eyelet affixed to the deck; used as a guide for lines

Cleat: small T-like projection from the deck used to secure lines

Coaming: cockpit sides above the deck line

Cockpit: the helm; also open deck sections for passengers

Companionway: steps leading below from the deck

Cradle: wooden framework used for onshore boat support

Cuddy: small cabin under foredeck of a runabout

Deck: floor of the boat

Displacement: weight of the boat, measured as the total amount of water displaced by the hull

Draft: depth of the hull from waterline to keel

Ebb tide: outgoing tide

Eddy: circular swirl of water

Even keel: properly trimmed

Fast: secured

Fathom: six feet of water depth

Fenders: cushions along the outside of the boat

Flood tide: incoming tide

Flybridge: cockpit mounted above the regular cockpit; used for better visibility and deepsea fishing

Following sea: waves approaching

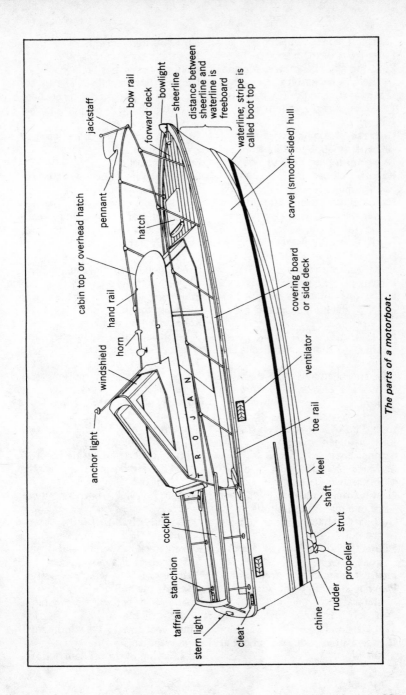

The parts of a motorboat.

from the rear of the boat

Fore: front of the boat (bow)

Fore-and-aft: Lengthwise: opposite of athwartships

Freeboard: length of the boat sides above the waterline

Galley: kitchen

Grab rails: hand holds

Grapnel: small, hooked anchor

Gunwale: topmost rail or side

Hatch: deck opening

Head: toilet

Helm: pilot's control station; also the steering machinery, including rudder and wheel

Hitch: easily loosened knot

Hold: interior of the boat

Hull: shell of the boat

Inboard: within or part of the hull

Keel: runs along the bottom center of the hull; backbone of the boat

Knot: measure of water speed; equal to one nautical mile per hour

Lee: area sheltered from the wind

Leeward: direction away from the wind

Line: boat rope

List: slant of a boat to one side

Lurch: sudden rolling

Marina: boat basin

Midships: broadest part of a ship

Moor: secure a boat

Nautical mile: equal to 6,080 feet or one minute of latitude

Outboard: attached to or outside the hull

Painter: mooring line of a small boat

Pitch: fore-and-aft motion

Planing: skimming the surface of the water

Port: left side of the boat, looking toward the bow

Quarter: either side of the boat at the aft

Rib: hull frame member

Rode: anchor line or cable

Roll: sideways motion

Rudder: vertical fin attached to the hull behind the propeller; turns the boat by pushing the stern sideways

Running lights: nighttime navigation lights

Screw: propeller

Scupper: hole allowing water to run off the deck

Sea anchor: cone-shaped device trailed from the stern to keep the boat heading into the wind

Sheer: the top edge of the deck or rail

Skeg: stabilizing fin usually supporting the rudder

Starboard: right side of the boat, facing the bow

Stern: rear end of the boat

Superstructure: all the structure above the deck

Tiller: steering handle attached to the outboard motor (or rudder)

Topside: above the waterline

Transom: back of boat across the stern from which the outboard motor is hung

Trim: manner of floating according to arrangement of weight and/or sail

Trough: cavity between two waves

Underbody: hull below the waterline

Wake: track of waves and foam left astern of a moving boat

Waterline: line at which the water meets the hull

Weather: direction from which the wind blows

Windward: toward the wind; same as weather

Yaw: swing of an off-course boat

CHAPTER THREE
Motors

■ One aspect of the sport of boating that can prove to be a source of great confusion can very well be in the choosing of the right motor with which to power your boat. The choice of what motor to buy is most critical and must be made with great care. If you should have a motor installed which is too small for the size boat you possess, the motor will have to perform more work than it should for efficient operation. This overworking of the motor will cause it to be subject to more-than-necessary visits to the repair shop which, in turn, means less-than-possible time in the water and unnecessarily high expenses. By overworking the motor, you will also give it a shorter life than it otherwise would have. On the other hand, should you purchase a motor too large for the boat you own, you'll be wasting your money because you'll be buying power you don't need. Not only that but you could very well cause damage to be done to the hull of your boat. The overpowerful motor could make the boat go faster than its design was meant to go. Acquiring the proper balanced relationship between boat and motor is no simple matter. The best source of authorita-

tive information is probably a reputable boat dealer . . . and you should try to find the most reputable dealer around before buying either a boat or a motor. However, it would be wise to be aware of at least the basics used in correctly meshing boat and motor before approaching a dealer.

OUTBOARDS

In the beginning, outboard motors were developed to be used as devices for propelling small boats. Obviously, they were invented by some ingenious individual who had grown tired of pulling a pair of oars in order to move from one place on the water to another. Also, the original outboard motors were extremely portable and could be taken along on almost any trip to where small craft would be available for hire. Since those early days, though, outboards have done a considerable amount of growing up. Today, there are outboard motors which can be purchased that have as many as 150 hp. Generally speaking, so-called small boats, those up to about twenty-three feet in length, are powered by outboard motors.

Almost all outboard motors are

25

two-cycle, water-cooled power plants. The word "almost" is used because there is one exception to this generalization of the outboard. That one exception is a four-cycle outboard made by Homelite. For the benefit of the newcomer to the world of engines, a two-cycle means that out of every two strokes of the piston, one stroke is a power stroke. Following that logic, the Homelite four-cycle has one of every four piston strokes as a power stroke. However, let's stick with the overwhelming rule as it applies to outboard motors.

These motors call for oil to be mixed directly in the cylinder with the gasoline (all standardly produced outboard motors are fueled by gasoline). The ratio of oil to gasoline varies, depending on the manufacturer of the engine. When the oil-gasoline mixture reaches the cylinder, the gasoline vaporizes and burns away, providing the propelling power. However, the oil remains to perform its task of lubricating the cylinder, the walls of the crankcase, the engine bearings, and all other moving parts. To get a fairly accurate estimate of how much gasoline is consumed by an outboard engine, divide the number of horsepower at which the engine is rated by ten. The resulting answer will be the approximate number of gallons of gasoline that will be consumed by your boat in a period of one hour while operating at full throttle.

The advent of the outboard motor has most certainly been the major reason for the boom in the boating industry. Outboards account for more than half of all the powered pleasure boats sold in the United States. And there are approximately eight million (8,000,000) of these craft floating around! There was a time when, in its early years, the outboard was almost more trouble than it was worth. While its small size and extreme portability made it rather a simple task to get it to a repair shop, the early outboard was noisy, smoky and in need of a trip to the repair shop far too often. But such is not the case today. The modern-day outboard is an extremely dependable piece of equipment . . . pleasing to the eye and a real pleasure to operate. While many of the outboards have lost their portability (a seventy-five horsepower model can weigh upwards of 240 pounds), they can perform at wide-open speeds without fear of conking out for as long as the fuel holds out. Very rarely is it the engine's fault when there is trouble with it . . . more often than not the trouble will be caused by low-quality or dirty

The outboard motor; powerful, efficient.

fuel, a fouled sparkplug, or the negligence of the owner. There are a variety of outboards available on the market today. There are one-cylinder models which can supply up to 7.5 horsepower; there are two-cylinder models, which are generally less noisy than the one-cylinder models, which can provide up to 55 hp; and there are three-cylinder motors which usually range from 60 to 85 hp. These generally have an electric starter as optional available equipment.

When used on small utility boats, outboards tend to limit the boat's performance by putting extra weight on the boat's stern. However, the advantages gained by the use of an outboard on a boat of this type far outweigh the slight loss in performance. Since the entire motor is turned in the desired direction, the boat can very easily and almost unerringly be steered by the individual manning the helm. Even a young child can be quickly taught to properly steer a boat powered by an outboard motor. Of equal importance, the motor can be tilted upwards when running in rather shallow water to prevent grounding the boat and damaging the propeller. This ability to tilt the entire motor upward becomes an advantage of utmost importance when it is necessary or desirable to ground a boat, as in beaching. And not to be overlooked is the advantage of being able to completely remove the outboard and take it along with you when leaving the boat. This, more than anything else you could do, prevents the motor from being stolen. Still another

important factor in favor of the outboard is that it avoids a problem which is an inherent feature in other types of motors. Being completely on the outside of the boat, any gasoline leaks and excess fumes are absorbed and removed by the water and atmosphere. This prevents fumes being able to collect to cause fire or explosion. Of course, easy maintenance is possible because an outboard presents its motor openly.

The following table is provided as a guide with which to judge the need for outboard power in relation to boat size. It cannot be emphasized too strongly that horsepower depends on a variety of factors, such as hull design and the weight-load of the boat to be propelled:

Overall Boat Length x Transom Width

30'	80'	120'
40'	90'	130'
50'	100'	140'
60'	110'	145'
70'		

Maximum Safe Horsepower

3	70	150
5	90	170
15	110	190
30	130	200
50		

INBOARDS

A boat with an inboard motor differs from an outboard craft in that it has a propeller and rudder which are permanently fixed, whereas the outboard is readily removable. This severely limits the water depth at which the inboard can be safely run. Should the inboard be run into too shallow waters, the propeller could easily be caused to come into contact with the bottom which would certainly result in its being damaged.

However, inboards are not built to be used in small boats which go into shallow waters. The inboard is quite appropriately known as the big daddy of boating. There is virtually no limit to the power available with inboards. Like the outboard, the inboard engine is water-cooled, drawing upon the water surrounding it for cooling rather than making use of a closed, recirculating system such as the one ordinarily used in the family automobile. Inboards, as the name implies, are inserted into the body of the boat. Therefore, they must be equipped with bilge blowers to prevent any gasoline leaks and excess fumes from accumulating and causing fire and/or explosion.

The standard inboard motor, as all other types of powered motors used in boating, has only one gear for moving the boat in a forward direction. It also features, as standard equipment, a neutral gear to be used when not moving either forward or backward, and a reverse gear for moving backward. The reverse gear is also used as the boat's only possible means of braking, should it be desirable to come to a quick stop while moving in a forward direction. Inboard motors can also be purchased with an optional piece of equipment called a reduction gear.

This is a device which reduces the number of revolutions of the motor in transmitting power from the engine to the propeller. This, in turn, permits the propeller to revolve at its most efficient rate. In other words, a smaller engine can be used than would otherwise be needed if the reduction gear were not a part of its equipment. By doing this, greater efficiency is achieved while cutting down on the initial cost of buying a larger-than-needed engine and cutting down on the continual cost of using more fuel than necessary.

The horsepower range of inboard motors for pleasure boats ranges from a 15 hp used for small auxiliary boats all the way up to approximately a 415 hp for the really big motor yachts that need that much power to move them through the water. Unfortunately, there are many unwise boatmen who buy these big jobs for smaller boats that do not need them. Inboards can be generally categorized as being heavy-duty, medium-duty, and high-speed. However, bracketing these by their horsepower rating really has no meaning or purpose at all. Rather, it is the ratio of horsepower to hull design, size, and weight which is the determining factor as to what category in which to place an inboard. While the preceding chart indicated a somewhat rough approximation of the maximum horsepower which an outboard boat can safely accommodate, no such chart is practical for inboard motors. There are simply too many combinations possible.

When considering the purchase

Marine Diesel; strong, economical.

of an inboard, there is something besides the horsepower to be considered. There is a choice to be made between a gasoline-fueled engine or a diesel engine. They are both internal combustion engines. That is, they both transmit power by getting air and fuel into their cylinders where they ignite the mixture. The difference between the two engines lies in their relative compression. In the more popular gasoline engine, the mixture of air and fuel is first blended by a carburetor and then drawn into the cylinders where it is compressed by pistons and ignited by an electric spark thrown off by a spark plug. This sequence of events is different in a diesel engine. The diesel's cylinder draws in only air, no fuel. This eliminates the need for a carburetor. The air is compressed to a much greater degree than in the gasoline engine which results in a much higher temperature. At the moment when the air reaches its highest temperature; diesel fuel is automatically injected into the cylinder. The fuel is instantly vaporized and ignites spontaneously by the extreme heat of the compressed air. This makes it unnecessary for the diesel engine to have spark plugs.

In view of the fact that the diesel engine has a fewer number of parts and burns far less costly

fuel, a question quite logically comes to mind. How come all stock outboard motors and a great majority of inboard engines are designed to use gasoline as fuel? Why hasn't the diesel completely taken over the boat engine market? The answer lies in the weight of the diesel, its size, and its initial cost. The parts of a diesel engine have to be heavier than those of a comparable gasoline engine because of the greater pressure produced by the diesel's higher compression. Being heavier, they are also more expensive. Also, its heavier weight and larger size also makes it less desirable for most pleasure boats. Of course, if the boat is used frequently enough over a long enough period of time, the savings in the cost of fuel will compensate for the greater initial expense. But few pure pleasure boats are used that frequently or over a long enough period of time. For that reason, diesels find the welcome mat out almost exclusively among boats involved in commercial fishing and among the luxurious, large motor yachts that are big in weight and size and where high initial costs are not a problem. As the boat salesman said to the shopper who asked the price of a motor yacht, "Sir, if you have to ask the price, you can't afford it."

STERNDRIVES

While the gasoline-fueled inboard motor was already quite popular way back in the early 1900's, the sterndrive or I.O. (inboard outdrive) did not come into any kind of prominence until around 1960. However, it has become quite popular since then and will undoubtedly keep its place in the scheme of things as long as we continue to have boating.

Sterndrives are a cross between inboard and outboard motors and give their owners what could be considered the best of both engine worlds. They combine the advantages of the inboard's reliability, power, and relative fuel economy with the outboard's advantages of being portable, being tiltable, and causing minimal underwater drag. Basically, a sterndrive is an inboard engine which is located at the extreme aft end of the boat and is coupled to an outboard-type drive through the transom. This drive unit is called an outdrive.

Like the standard outboard, the outdrive provides the distinct advantage of being able to be tilted. This permits the boat to which it is attached to be beached or run through relatively shallow water. It is also generally possible to crank the outdrive completely up out of the water so that a fouled propeller can be cleared by someone in the boat; this also makes it possible to replace a propeller which has been somehow damaged. The outdrive can also be completely detached from the inboard engine and taken to a repair shop should this be necessary or kept out of the water to prevent water corrosion in the event the boat is not to be used for several days but still left in the water. Of course, should there be a problem with the inboard engine, then the problem is exactly the same as with a total inboard. The repair work would have to be done either aboard the boat or the entire boat would have to be hauled out of the water and transported to the repair shop.

One important factor which must be taken into account when considering the purchase of a sterndrive is the design of the boat in which it is to be installed. Being that the engine is installed in the extreme aft end of the boat, determination must be made as to whether or not the boat can safely accommodate the weight without having its rear dangerously and/or uneconomically dragged. When buying a new boat which has been specifically designed for a sterndrive, this factor has already been taken into account; however, this factor must be carefully checked out when considering installing a sterndrive in a boat you already own or into a boat that was not

Sterndrives are gaining favor among proponents of both inboards and outboards.

initially designed for this type of propulsion.

JET ENGINES

Basically, jet engines propel the boats to which they are affixed in the same manner as do all other types of engines. That is, the boat is moved forward by a stream of water forced outward from the stern. However, there is one major difference between all other engines and the jet . . . there is no exposed propeller churning the water on the outside of the boat powered by a jet engine. Instead, the propeller is completely enclosed in the turbine-like housing of the motor.

Jet engines generally range in power from 155 hp to 450 hp and have become extremely popular among our more affluent boatmen, especailly those who favor water skiing and skin diving as water sports. Being that there is no exposed, churning propeller to be concerned with, skiiers and divers can safely board the boat from the stern, which is more stable, than from either side. Jet engines are generally of the outboard type and are available as either air-cooled or water-cooled.

PROPELLERS

No matter which type engine you use for powering your boat with the exception of the jet, it will have a propeller which will do just that which the name of this piece of equipment implies . . . it propels the craft through the water.

As much as it would be desirable to have, there is no table which can be devised to gauge the correct propeller for your boat and motor . . . such as the table which can be used as a guide for matching boat length and maximum safe horsepower of an outboard motor. The working efficiency of a propeller is completely dependent upon the shape of the hull and the weight of the boat as well as the load the boat will carry, and the size and type of motor driving the prop. Putting similar motors and similar propellers on hulls having dissimilar shapes can result in tremendously varying performances of all.

Without the addition of reduction gears, it requires the use of a large motor to turn a large propeller rather than a small motor. The engineering basis of engine power, and hence propeller thrust, is the relative rpm (revolutions per minute). A large motor builds up more force, or torque, per rpm than does a small motor. Therefore, a large motor is more capable of turning a heavy, large propeller against the natural resistance of the water by which it is surrounded. But large motors are more expensive to buy and operate than are smaller motors. That's why reduction gears are looked upon with so much favor by wise buyers of motors.

Propellers are available in either right-handed or left-handed versions. This means that, when viewed from astern, they rotate either clockwise or counter-clockwise. Most propellers manufactured for use by the boating industry are the right-handed variety. Also, it has been found that having the tops of the propeller blades curl outward aids in maneuvering. ●

CHAPTER FOUR

The Hull:
Designs and Materials

■ A boat's performance is determined far more by the design of her hull than by any other single factor. Unless the lines of the hull are correctly designed to give the desired performance, the boat will be a "lemon" no matter how many horsepower is supplied by the engine, whether inboard, outboard, or sterndrive. There is no way in which a large engine will properly move a boat if the hull lines were not drawn right while they were still on the naval architect's drawing board. The experienced boat owner pays a great deal of attention to the design of his hull and feels it is well worth the price of using the services of a good naval architect who will know just how to draw the lines for the type of boat he wants to have built.

While there are quite a number of types of hulls, there are really only two general classes into which all types of hulls fall . . . the displacement hull and the planing hull. All the other types are simply modifications of one or the other, or a combination of both.

DISPLACEMENT HULLS

The displacement hulls are very logically and correctly so named because, as they plough their way through the water, they actually displace their own weight of water. The designated weight of a displacement-hull boat is determined by calculating the weight of the water it displaces. In other words, a boat listed as a 12,000-ton vessel wouldn't weigh in at 12,000 tons were it somehow to be lifted out of the water and placed on a land-based scale. Rather, this listing really means that the boat's hull displaces 12,000 tons of water as it goes on its merry way.

There is a measured limit to the speed that a boat fitted with a pure displacement hull can attain. This limit is imposed by the length of the hull at its waterline. The most efficient displacement hull built can not be induced to go any faster than the square root of its waterline length multiplied by 1.25. As an example to help explain this theory, let us assume a displacement hull which measures out at a length of twenty-five feet at the waterline. Now, as all mathemeticians know, the square root of twenty-five is five. By multiplying five by 1.25, we find that this particular hull will go no faster than 6.25 knots per hour. And it doesn't matter how much power is put in back of this hull . . . its speed will just never go beyond the 6.25 knots per hour. That's all the speed you can justifiably expect to get. Once this speed has been attained, there is no advantage to be gained by opening the throttle any further. The extra power which is generated by this act will only be wasted in the creation of a bigger wave astern. Another disadvantage of trying to overdrive a displacement hull is that the hull can readily become more difficult to handle properly. Of course, the waterline rule continues to apply even when the boat is heavily-laden with extra cargo. Using the same amount of power, there would be no appreciable decrease in the speed of the boat. You see, by increasing the load in the boat, you cause the boat to ride lower in the water (you increase its draft). This, in turn, increases the length of the hull at the waterline which increases its displacement, thereby compensating for the additional weight.

A displacement hull slices its way through water with as little tumult as possible. Any surface waves through which it goes have very little if any effect on the performance of this type of hull. This is because the major bulk of the hull is traveling at a depth below the waves. As a general rule, displacement hulls will give performances in rough water than can easily be rated as superior. It can travel at almost full speed through heavy seas and is easier to hold on course and easier to handle in winds than any other type of hull design.

In addition to improving its stability, the long, deep keel of a displacement-hull boat allows for more ample cabin space below its deck. This displacement hull is ideal for the boatman who desires a cruiser with spacious room and long range capabilities. It is also the perfect choice for the fisherman who is more concerned with having a seaworthy hull under him than he is with speed.

PLANING HULLS

Whereas the displacement hull slices its way *through* the water, the planing hull skims along the *surface* of the water. There is no real limit to the speed which a planing hull can attain since it is not restricted by any bulk of its hull being down in the water and meeting the water's resistance. Because the planing hull has relatively flat surfaces, which are generally broad, flat areas toward the stern of the boat, the boat will actually be lifted, when traveling at high speed; this lifting action is what causes the planing hull to skim the surface of the water.

Until the boat achieves the velocity known as its "planing speed", it is actually a displacement hull. But once enough speed

A planing hull rides the surface.

is attained to lift the hull up to the surface and it starts to skim along, it will go faster and faster as more horsepower is brought into action. The more power supplied, the faster the boat will travel. Actually, the only limits to the speed which a planing hull can be powered to are those imposed upon it by the friction of the surface water and the added friction of the air surrounding its raised bulk. The speed which the planing hull must reach before it can begin to life to skim along the surface of the water is somewhat more than fifteen miles per hour. Operating a boat with a planing hull at less than planing speed will cause it to be somewhat difficult to handle properly. This is because a planing hull is considerably lighter and relatively much flatter than a comparatively-sized displacement hull.

Generally speaking, the planing hull performs best in smooth water. Due to the fact that a pure planing hull skims along the surface of the water, it reacts more adversely to rough water than does the displacement hull. Just about every wave is capable of sending a shock through the boat. This can be most disadvantageous when boating in rough weather.

The speed of the boat has to be reduced in order to prevent the boat from being shaken to pieces. In other words, the planing hull has to be converted back to a displacement hull to keep it from being either broken up or swamped by really choppy waters. Yet, when the boat is slowed down to below planing speed, the boat becomes hard to control. So it would seem that planing hulls should only be used in calm, smooth water. And for the most part, that is true.

However, there really being virtually no limit to the ingenuity of man, this inability of the pure planing hull to handle choppy, open seas has resulted in modifications to this type of hull. One such design, used to a great extent for speedy runabouts, combines a displacement-type V-hull with the features of a planing hull. The flat, horizontal planing surface is shifted even further aft, with the V-hull forward. The result of this modification gives us a boat that is easier to handle on open, choppy water without too great a sacrifice in planing speed, although there is some natural loss in attained velocity in relation to power expended.

TYPES OF HULLS

Round Bottom: Round-bottom hulls are eminently seaworthy members of the displacement hull category. They have a graceful curve from the rail to the keel and are probably the oldest of all the hull designs. Because of their curvature, round-bottom hulls are not among the most easy to construct of hulls and are, therefore, somewhat in the expensive range. The more simple of these hulls feature curves which are convex. There is a more difficult to construct and, therefore, a more expensive form of the round-bottom hull known as the *compound* round-bottom hull. The compound combines both convex and concave curves in its design.

The curved design and the round bottom make this type of hull give a very comfortable ride. Having virtually no square or rectangular projections, it meets with little water resistance and is, therefore, quite easily propelled. This type of hull is heavily favored for use on low-speed fishing boats. A round-bottom hull has the added advantage of being quite strong. For this reason, it is the preferred type of hull for rough-water, open-seas cruisers and sailers.

Flat Bottom: This is another type of hull which falls into the general classification of a displacement hull. The flat-bottom hull is far and away the easiest type of hull to build and, therefore, the least expensive. A boat fitted with a flat-bottom hull is ideal for fishing on rivers or small lakes. In these waters and for that purpose, it is far more important that the boat have the ability to stay afloat in a normal position when someone in the boat rises to his feet to cast than it is to be speedy and have handling efficiency. Stability is preferred in these instances to high-performance.

Flat-bottoms are widely criticized as being more than just somewhat unseaworthy. And the adverse criticism is, to a great extent, justified. Generally speaking, these hulls have a tendency toward pounding badly when they are driven through choppy water . . . and they require an otherwise unnecessary amount of power to be moved. Again man's ingenuity enters upon the scene with the result that there are flat-bottom boats, such as certain dory modifications and garveys, which have little trouble in open water. Aside from these exceptions to the general rule, though, the flat-bottom is basically a shallow-water vessel which is most suitable for use in protected inland waterways. You will find flat-bottoms mostly used on small rowboats and fishing outboards.

V-Bottom: This type of hull is most aptly described by its name. It has sides which are almost straight as they come down at an angle chosen by the boat's designer. The sides end where they meet, depending on their angle of descent. Their point of intersection is called the chine. If the two sides meet to form a sharp edge, the hull is known as a hard chine; if the point of intersection is somewhat rounded, it is known as a soft chine.

While the sides of V-bottoms are virtually straight, there is some degree of curvature. A concave curve is used for powerboats to help them knife through the water while flattening the spray; a convex curve proves the softening feature of a round bilge. This is sometimes used for sailing boats.

Tri-hull: Compared to a V-hull, a tri-hull has a relatively flat bow. The use of a flat bow in the design

Tri-hulls utilize their increased bow width to great advantage.

allows for the opening up of the interior space which, in turn, provides additional seating and storage space. The tri-hull is also heavier than a V-hull and it offers a larger surface to the water. A tri-hull boat has an extremely high degree of stability. The extra space at the bow can well be utilized as a diving platform for those who like to swim out from and around a boat.

The tri-hull falls into the general classification of planing hulls. It is somewhat slower than a comparable V-hull in reaching planing speed. Because of the complexity of curves in their design, most generally tri-hulls are constructed of molded fiberglass. They find their greatest popularity when

The tunnel drive encompasses many new engineering advantages.

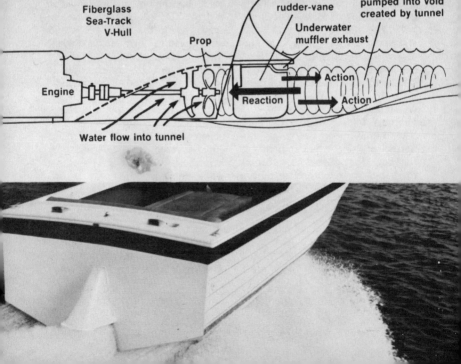

used for family-style runabouts.

Tunnel Drive: This is nothing more than a modified ordinary, deep V-hull. The modification consists of a hydrodynamic tunnel located just above the keel line. By having the propeller shaft placed within the tunnel, the boat can realize much better results in performance as well as greater speed . . . without the need to use a larger motor.

By examining most conventional inboard engines, it can readily be seen that the propeller shaft is installed at an angle. It can also be observed that a good deal of the water is driven downward by the propeller itself, dissipating quite a bit of its propelling power. The tunnel-drive works differently. Here, the propeller within the tunnel drives the propelled water horizontally. It can, therefore, be readily seen that an added push, or additional use of present power, is derived from the use of the tunnel. The operation of the tunnel-drive is quite simple. As the boat moves forward, there is a vacuum which is created within the tunnel. The water on the outside rushes in to fill this void with considerable force (nature, somehow, cannot tolerate a vacuum). As it does so, there is a tremendous amount of water forced into the tunnel . . . and onto the propeller.

A tunnel-drive hull will give good performance through improved forward steering. This is made possible by the rush of water against the rudder. The boat built with a tunnel-drive can also turn quickly even at slow speeds because of this relationship with the water. Developed only over the last several years, tunnel drives have been used successfully on runabouts.

MATERIALS USED IN HULL CONSTRUCTION

The most commonly used materials in the construction of boats are wood, steel, aluminum, and fiberglass. Conditions of the water in the locality in which you will be doing your boating plus the performance factors desired as well as your personal preferences should be carefully considered before making a choice as to which material will be used to build your boat. Another important and not to be overlooked factor is the cost of upkeep of the various hull construction materials.

Each of the above listed materials has its good points and its bad points. We will attempt to point out both for all the materials listed below.

WOOD

There is a natural sound-absorbing quality to wood and hulls made from this construction material seem to provide extra insulation against vibrations. Of course, there is nothing in this whole, wide world that can stand up to a hull made from wood when it comes to visual beauty, especially when the wood is given a final coat of natural varnish. This gives the wood a bright, lustrious finish. Wooden hulls have many advantages over hulls made from other materials. Wooden hulls feature a combination of lightness of weight with great intrinsic strength. Due to the fact that wood can be simply worked, a wooden hull is easier to build than any other type, requiring nothing more than relatively simple hand tools. However, granted that wood has all of these advantages, wood hulls are found chiefly on extremely expensive boats (where the cost is $50,000 and over) or, conversely, on extremely inexpensive boats.

This seeming contradiction in facts is due to the major disadvantage of using wood in the construction of a boat ... maintenance. A wooden boat can last an indeterminate period of time provided it has been properly designed, well constructed, meticulously cared for, and sufficiently ventilated. However, wood is an organic substance. Being organic, it is also porous. It shrinks and swells with changes in temperature and humidity and is subject to all sorts of maladies ... especially the spores of dry rot. They can deteriorate very rapidly and completely succumb to dry rot while resting during the off-season out of the water. Unless the wood is protected by an application of poisonous paint, wooden boats become easy targets of shipworms such as marine borers and teredo worms. The latter need only a very short time in which to work and they can transform a plank of wood into a riddled, hollow shell. As you can see, wooden hulls absolutely require a good deal of care ... especially periodic sanding and painting to protect them from infestations. Also, due to their facility for swelling and shrinking, wooden hulls will leak

for anywhere from a day to a week when they are put back into the water after having been kept out of water for a season. This leaking continues until the shrunken dry boards swell back again to their former watertight position.

There are a variety of woods available for use in hull construction. The most preferred woods for boat construction are Honduras mahogany or Port Oxford cedar for planking, white oak which has been properly seasoned is preferred for framing, and teak has the greatest preference for building decks. The mahogany and cedar mentioned above as well as several other grades of cedar, cypress and heavy yellow pine are noted for their resistancy to rot. Lignum vitae is also good for its worm resistancy but it is very heavy. Teak ranks exceedingly high in its resistance to rot and also to shipworms. However, it is very rare and extremely expensive. While seasoned white oak is a most desirable piece of lumber for boat building, avoid the use of red oak. This particular wood seems to have dry rot built into itself by the forces of nature. Currently, good white oak is in somewhat short supply so be on guard against having red oak substituted for the white oak you ordered. That's right, there are some nefarious materials dealers who would stoop to such low practices.

There are several ways in which wooden hulls are built. One of the most highly preferred construction methods is the use of solid planking in either one of two designs. One of the designs, known as the Carvel-built boat, has each plank lying flat, adjoining the next plank side-by-side, with enough clearance between the planks to allow for caulking and natural swelling. This method gives the hull a very smooth appearance. The other design is known as the Lapstrake. This design inherently avoids the need for caulking. In a lapstrake, each horizontal plank overlaps the plank directly beneath it, much like shingles overlap each other in housing construction. A hull designed this way will move more slowly through the water than a comparable carvel because its larger surface area causes it to have greater water friction. Another disadvantage of the lapstrake is that it is more difficult to sand and paint. It does, however, offer a softer ride than the carvel. Another wooden hull design is the Strip-built boat which is made up of narrow strips of wood rather than planks. The edge of each strip is marine-glued and nailed to the next strip.

There are, of course, hulls built of laminated wood. When large panels of laminated wood are used, the results are high degree of strength and lightness of weight. This type of construction is also fast and easy which means the manufacturer can cut his production costs and, therefore, cut his selling price. Boats built of laminated wood, as all other boats, should be adequately framed, well-joined at the point of intersection (or chine) and the keel. Of course, the lamination should be made of marine-grade panels.

STEEL

This metal has many favorable facets which should recommend it most highly for use in boat construction. Steel is very strong and is extremely durable; it has a low rate of upkeep when it is used properly regarding formula, thickness, and construction. A hull made of steel makes an ideal radio ground and provides great effective radiated power to telephones aboard ship; metal cabins offer passengers and crew within protection from lightning during electrical storms. Steel hulls, because of their intrinsic strength, are able to withstand severe pounding of waves. Yet, with all these favorable aspects, steel hulls are not generally used in modern-day, pleasure boat building. As with hulls constructed of other metals, steel hulls are subject to extreme noise and vibration. They must be sprayed on the inside with a sound-deadening material. Otherwise, the noise would be almost unbearable to passengers. Also, steel used in construction makes for heavy boats which are difficult to drydock. And probably the most important drawback to the use of steel in the construction of boats is the fact that it must be constantly maintained in order to prevent it from rusting.

ALUMINUM

When proper alloys are used, aluminum proves to be almost as strong as steel while being much lighter and more manageable than steel. An aluminum hull, built with modern marine alloys, rates very high in performance and also has a low-upkeep ratio. In addition, this type of hull has proven to have very little tendency toward corrosion. Aluminum boats must be constructed of special marine-grade alloys. Otherwise, salt-water electrolysis can decompose a boat within a week or so after its entry into the water. The process of electrolysis can be a most serious problem for all metal boats not properly protected. Sea water contains metallic salts which, under the current caused by an improperly grounded motor, can either replace or corrode the metal in a hull. Under proper conditions of construction, however, an aluminum hull offers the same advantages as steel as regards good radio ground and passenger protection during electrical storms.

Because it is light in weight, aluminum is often used in the manufacture of small, lightweight, inexpensive boats such as utility car-toppers. Most of these are fitted with a flotation device which prevents the boat from sinking should it be capsized. Any hull that does not float, such as those made of metal, fiberglass, and some types of molded plywood, should be equipped with some form of flotation device. Lightweight aluminum is extremely malleable. This permits it to be easily molded into pleasing-to-the-eye shapes, such as those employed in small runabouts. However, its very lightness proves to be a serious disadvantage once the aluminum boat is afloat. At the speeds generally used by runabouts, the bow tends to rise. Any sort of wind getting beneath the hull and exerting pressure thereon can make for difficulty in steering.

FIBERGLASS

There are many reasons why fiberglass is fast becoming one of the most popular materials used in the construction of boat hulls. For one thing, fiberglass is one of the most durable of the hull materials used and is one of the strongest. Fiberglass requires only minimal maintenance, as it is immune to shipworms and completely free from the risk of dry rot. A fiberglass hull, by eliminating the need for bulky frames, provides for maximum room below decks.

The list of advantages of using fiberglass continues by its making a one-piece hull which requires no seams ... therefore, no leaks. Should the fiberglass hull be somehow punctured, it can easily be repaired. If it should get scratched, as it undoubtedly would, it need not be retouched. Most fiberglass hulls are color impregnanged and scratches do now show up.

Although fiberglass weighs less than does wood, it is still a heavy material and makes for a rather relatively plain appearance. And, as mentioned earlier, fiberglass does not naturally float. Therefore, the hull should be fitted with flotation devices.

All things being considered, fiberglass has so many advantages its disadvantages are far outweighed, thus today, fiberglass is used in the construction of runabouts, motor yachts, and houseboats. ●

CHAPTER FIVE

Boating Equipment

■ There are actually three types of equipment which are used on boats. One type is the mandatory, which is all the equipment that is prescribed by law ... either federal, state, or both. Mandatory equipment *must* be carried on boats, according to their class (to be explained a bit further on). Another type of equipment is that which is deemed as being the minimum equipment to be carried on board and is known as *necessary* equipment. The third type is known as *optional* equipment. While not required by law and not absolutely necessary in many instances, to the proper functioning of the boat, these pieces of equipment are those things which are carried aboard for the primary sake of convenience. The boat may not run any better or be any safer with these things aboard, but the time spent afloat may be more enjoyable because of them.

MANDATORY EQUIPMENT

All the "navigable" waters of the United States are under control of the federal government. These are the waterways which are, in fact, navigable by boats engaged in international or interstate travel and/or trade. Included in this category of waterways are the coastal portions on both the Atlantic and Pacific Ocean sides of the United States, the Missis-

sippi River, and the Great Lakes. Should you have any doubt regarding whether or not the waters you will be using fall into this category, consult your local Coast Guard office or write a letter to the U.S. Coast Guard, Washington, D.C.

Should the waters you will be boating on fall into the "non-navigable" category, such as Lake Hopatcong in New Jersey or the Salton Sea in California, individual state laws will be the determining factor as to what *must* be on board. There are instances where a state may also have specific requirements regarding boating on navigable waterways. These will always be concurrent with federal standards as state laws can in no way be in conflict with or can they in any way diminish the requirements of the federal government on any waterways under federal jurisdiction. The Motorboat Act of 1940 is the legislation which basically regulates what equipment must be aboard any boat plying federally controlled waterways. The provisions of this act still remain in effect though we now have the Federal Boat Safety Act of 1971 as its basic source of authority. Federal equipment requirements can be found in a small pamphlet known as Publication CG-258 "Rules and Regulations for Undocumented Vessels." This pamphlet can be obtained without charge from all Coast Guard District offices or from Headquarters, U.S. Coast Guard, Washington, D.C. 20591. Regarding boating on non-navigable waterways, consult your local state Department of Recreation, or other state agency concerned with these matters, for a list of that state's requirements concerning any mandatory equipment for your particular boat.

The minimum equipment that must be carried aboard as required by federal statutes varies, depending on what class your motorboat falls into; class is determined by length. You can find the length of your boat, and thereby its class, by running a straight, level measuring line from end to end of the hull along the deck or where the deck would be in case there is no deck. This should be done from bow to stern parallel to the centerline. The federal government's regulations divide boats into four classes. They are:

Class A: less than 16 feet

Class 1: 16 feet to less than 26 feet

Class 2: 26 feet to less than 40 feet

Class 3: 40 feet to not more than 65 feet

The list of items of equipment required by the law is rather surprisingly small. However, there is little or no flexibility to the equipment required and the items are very clearly specified. Most items must be classified as "approved." Boat owners should, for their own sake and the sake of any passengers they may have on board, always consider that the mandatory requirements are mere minimum standards. In other words, if federal regulations require that a particular boat must carry two fire extinguishers, the owner should examine his boat most carefully. Are two extinguishers really adequate for complete safety? Will they be located where one would be available for adequate protection regardless where in the boat a fire may happen? While two extinguishers would fulfill the letter of the law and satisfy the authorities, it might well be more desirable and even necessary, because of the layout of a specific craft, to carry three or more. True safety should always be of greater consideration for boat owners than mere compliance with the minimum requirements of the law. The following is a list of federally-required equipment:

LIFESAVING EQUIPMENT

All motorboats under the jurisdiction of the United States Coast Guard are required to carry at least one lifesaving device, of an approved type, for each person on board. These devices must be readily accessible by each such passenger. "Persons on board" takes in any persons being towed by the boat, such as skiers. There are a number of different types of lifesaving devices available. These must meet certain specifications, or exceed them, before they are listed as approved by the Coast Guard. There are lists of approved products published periodically. Some of these devices are:

Life preservers are probably the safest, and therefore the best, of all lifesaving devices. They come in two distinct styles: jacket and bib. These are generally constructed of a flotation material such as kapok or fibrous glass, enclosed in a cover of cloth to which is attached necessary straps and ties. A life preserver of either design, in order to be approved, must be able to support a person in the water in an upright or slightly backward position. It must also provide enough support to his head so that his face is held up above the water line even if he should become totally exhausted or lose consciousness. In order to win approval from Coast Guard inspectors, a life preserver must have the capability of getting its wearer into the described position, no matter what his position may have been when he entered the water.

Life rings or ring life buoys, which look like oversized doughnuts, have the capability of being easily and accurately thrown to someone who has somehow gone overboard. Acceptable construction materials are cork, balsa wood, and unicellular plastic. The outside of the doughnut-like ring is surrounded by a light rope which is fastened at four points to the ring. This is called a "grabline" and is used to provide a better grasp of the ring. The officially approved sizes of these rings are 20", 24", and 30" in diameter. There are usually rings of smaller diameters used for decorating the sides of boats. However, these smaller ones cannot be counted

toward the minimum number of lifesaving devices required by law.

The prudent boatman uses approved "yoke" type buoyant vest.

Buoyant vests are constructed of the same basic materials as are life preservers. There are a variety of designs which are in the "approved" class and these vests may be colored to fit the taste of the individual boat owner. Vests are somewhat smaller than life preservers and afford the wearer a bit less buoyancy. This makes them somewhat less safe but they are more comfortable. Of course, vests must be designed so that the wearer will float in the same position as that which is provided by the use of life preservers. Otherwise, the vest will not be officially approved and will not count toward the minimum legal requirement. Vests are only approved for use on boats classified as Class A, Class 1, and Class 2. They are not on the approved list for use on Class 3 boats nor can they be used on any class boat which carries passengers for hire. Life preservers, on the other hand, are approved for use in any boat of all classes.

A handy emergency flotation aid is a U.S. coast guard approved boat cushion.

Buoyant cushions are probably used on small boats to a greater extent than any other lifesaving device . . . and are the least desirable of all from a pure safety point of view. Cushions provide a greater degree of buoyancy than does a buoyant vest and therefore affords an adequate amount of flotation support. However, this applies only to a person in the water who is fully conscious and in complete control of the situation in which he finds himself. Cushions will not be of any safety value to a person who is exhausted or unconscious. These devices are the choice of many skippers of small boats because of their relatively low cost and also because they are easily stored due to their size and flat shape. Also, and unwisely, these cushions often serve the double purpose of being used as sitting cushions. This is a very unwise practice because cushions eventually lose their buoyancy when sat on over a

period of time. One alternative to this destruction of buoyancy is to store the cushions in an accessible area but where they will not be used to soften a passenger's seat; another alternative, and the least desirable, is to carefully inspect the cushions periodically and to replace them as soon as they show signs of being battered. Approved for use on Class A, Class 1, and Class 2, buoyant cushions are not approved for use on boats in Class 3 or on any class boat which carries fare-paying passengers.

The Federal Boat Safety Act of 1971 clearly requires that all manner of vessels, such as sail boats, craft propelled by oars, etc., must be equipped with the same number and type of lifesaving devices as prescribed for motorboats of the same length. The lifesaving equipment on any and all boats must be located so that it is easily accessible and must be in a constant state of good and serviceable condition. Any device not adhering to this requirement cannot and will not be counted toward the minimum number required for the specific boat in question.

While it is true that lifesaving equipment is rarely used on a boat (with a fair degree of luck it is *never* used), it is the most important item of equipment on board at that harrowing moment when it is needed. Therefore, the responsible owner of a boat will not hesitate to equip his craft with the very best lifesaving device available. The difference in initial cost between an absolutely safe and dependable life preserver and a somewhat less safe and dependable buoyant vest or cushion makes the purchase of life preservers a very sound investment in safety.

Those boatmen who go fishing or cruising, even on an irregular basis, in cold waters should give serious thought to buying a life raft as supplementary lifesaving equipment. Survival time in the water is reduced to a tremendous degree by the extemely low temperatures of northern waters and even the very best of life preservers may not be sufficient to keep a person afloat long enough to be rescued before he has succumbed to the cold. The best protection for circumstances such as these is a raft outfitted with a canopy which will not only keep a person out of the cold water but will also protect him from biting wind, blinding rain, etc. Again, it is to be sincerely hoped that this piece of equipment will never, never be needed. But what tremendous peace of mind can be yours when you know you have it if it should be needed.

FIRE EXTINGUISHERS

Fire extinguishing equipment is required on board almost every boat afloat. The only exception is an open outboard which is smaller than twenty-six feet in length. When there is no fixed fire extinguishing system installed in the boat's machinery space(s), portable fire extinguishers must be used in accordance with federal regulations. The number and type of extinguishers to be used are as follows: All Class A and Class 1 boats must carry at least one B-I type-approved hand portable extinguisher; Class 2 boats must be equipped with at least two B-I type-approved hand portable extinguishers; as an alternative, Class 2 boats may be equipped with at least one B-II type-approved hand portable extinguisher; Class 3 boats must carry at least three B-I type-approved hand portable extinguishers; or at least one B-I type plus one B-II type-approved hand portable extinguisher.

When there has been a fixed fire extinguishing system installed in the boat's machinery space(s), the following additional portable extinguishers must be carried aboard: on Class A and Class 1 boats, none; on Class 2 boats, at least one B-I type-approved hand portable extinguisher; on Class 3 boats, at least two B-I type-approved hand portable extinguishers or at least one B-II type-approved hand portable extinguisher.

B-I extinguishers contain the following ingredients: 1¼ to 2¼ gallons of foam, or 4 to 15 pounds of carbon dioxide, or 2 to 10 pounds of dry chemical. B-II extinguishers contain the following ingredients: 2½ gallons of foam, or 15 pounds of carbon dioxide, or 10 to 20 pounds of dry chemical.

As you can readily see, there are various kinds of fire extinguishers. Extinguishers which are approved for use on boats are described in terms of the ingredients which are the extinguishing agents. The different kinds of extinguishers are:

Dry chemical extinguishers are very popular because they are convenient to use and have a relatively low cost. To recharge a dry chemical extinguisher, all one has to do is to replace the discharged cylinder with a new cylinder. This is simply accomplished by merely screwing the new cylinder onto the discharge nozzle and valve assembly. This is most convenient and also permits spare cylinders to be carried on board for added safety should there be an outbreak of fire. Inside the cylinder is a dry chemical which is in a powdered form. When needed, this chemical is brought to bear on fire by a propellant gas which is under pressure. In order to obtain Coast Guard approval, these extinguishers must be fitted with a gauge which indicates the pressure existing inside the cylinder.

Carbon dioxide extinguishers have the advantage of not leaving any messy residue to be cleaned up after use. Also, they cannot damage the insides of engines as other types of extinguishers may. This is the type of extinguisher which must be used wherever a fixed fire extinguishing system is installed. Portable types of these extinguishers are made up of a cylinder which contains the gas (CO_2) under high pressure, a valve, and a short hose at the end of which is a discharge nozzle. These cylinders must be checked periodically, at least once a year to make sure the charge of extinguishing agent is sufficient for its purpose. This checking should be done by a qualified technician. Should the discharge be below required standards, the cylinder must be recharged. This servicing must not be overlooked. Lives

may very well depend on the extinguisher working properly. At the very least, valuable property can be seriously damaged or even totally destroyed because an efficient fire extinguisher was not available.

Foam extinguishers, while perfectly legal and acceptable for use on boats, are rarely if ever used on vessels of any class. They are notorious for leaving a messy residue that is extremely difficult to clean up and they are capable of causing damage to engine parts. Foam extinguishers do not make use of pressure as a propellant before use and they do not have to be checked for pressure leakage. As they do contain water, they must be checked against and protected from freezing. This type of extinguisher should be totally discharged and recharged on an annual basis.

There are several types of fire extinguishers which are quite effective for fighting fires but are not approved for use on boats because they are capable of producing highly poisonous gases. These non-acceptable types are the vaporizing-liquid types of extinguishers such as those containing carbontetrachloride and chlorobromonmethane. Extinguishers of this type should not even be carried on board as excess equipment. They present a danger to the health, possibly the very life, of anyone using them in confined areas.

To maintain a satisfactory level of safety on your boat, it is not enough to merely satisfy the letter of the law by buying and installing a sufficient number of fire extinguishers and then completely ignoring them until that unlikely but always possible terrifying moment when they are needed. They should be checked and maintained properly and periodically. All persons who regularly use the boat as well as visitors should be aware of the location of the apparatus and know how to use the extinguishers.

Back-fire Flame Arresters must be installed on every inboard gasoline

Flame arresters attach to carburetors to control flame of engine backfire.

engine. Commonly known as a "flame arrester", it is attached to the air intake of the carburetor to control any flame caused by the backfiring of the engine. These mechanical devices must be approved by the Coast Guard for use aboard motorboats and those that meet official specifications are designated as being approved for marine use. If the flame arrester you contemplate buying does not bear this designation, do not buy it for use on board your boat. Flame arresters should be securely attached to the carburetor's air intake with an absolutely air-tight connection. All its elements should be clean and there should

not be any separation in the grids that would allow passage to any flame.

Ventilators are required to air the lower portion of a boat's interior so as to prevent explosive vapors from collecting and presenting a hazard. All motor boats, except completely open craft, are required to have at least two ventilation ducts for each of its engines and fuel tank compartments ... one duct for an intake and the other for an exhaust. These ducts must be installed so that they lead from areas where vapors and fumes are most likely to collect, out to open air. Flexible plastic tubing which is impervious to acids and oil makes an easily-handled and durable duct to remove potentially dangerous gasoline vapors. As stated above, completely open boats are excluded from the federal regulations governing ventilators. However, there are very few boats which meet the Coast Guard's definition of an open boat. If you have any question at all as to whether your boat falls into this excluded class or not, install ventilators. You are much safer with them than otherwise.

Whistles and Bells are also required pieces of equipment. Much the same as all other equipment which is required by federal regulation, the requirements are set according to the size of the craft. Class A boats do not require any whistle at all; a Class 1 boat must be equipped with either a mouth, hand-operated, or power-operated whistle whose blast can be heard clearly at a distance of at least

Hand-held air horns are convenient, efficient signal-sounding devices.

one-half mile; a Class 2 craft must be equipped with either a hand-operated or a power-operated whistle (mouth whistles are not considered adequate for boats larger than Class 1) whose blast is audible at a distance of at least one mile; Class 3 boats are limited to using a power-operated whistle capable of emitting a sound which is audible at least one mile away. All whistles must be capable of having their blasts held for at least two seconds. Bells are not required for boats in Class A or Class 1, but Class 2 and Class 3 craft must be equipped with at least one bell which is capable of producing a clear, bell-like tone of full rounded characteristics. Although Coast Guard regulations do not require the use of a bell on boats in Class A or Class 1 and do not require the use of a whistle on Class A boats, these smaller boats are still required to sound proper whistle and fog signals by the Rules of the Road. Of course, just plain common sense and ordinary courtesy dictate that all boats, regardless of size, carry efficient signal-sounding equipment.

LIGHTS

Federal law requires that specifically-colored and specifically-located lights be displayed on all motorboats while they are underway or while they are anchored anywhere outside of federal anchorage areas, between the hours of sunset to sunrise. A boat is considered to be underway at any time it is not riding at anchor, it is not docked, or it is not aground. No other lights except those which are prescribed may be displayed as to do so would be misleading to other skippers. If the boat is outside federal waterways, the boat may be lighted according to International Rules which apply on the open sea. States, of course, may have their own set of lighting rules for their own "non-navigable" waterways.

The law requires that lights be visible for a specified arc when seen from certain directions. The angle of light is measured in terms of points, each point being equal to 11¼ nautical degrees. A completely open, naked light shines in 32 points which is the equivalent to a full circle. If a light is 10 points, then its arc is 10/32nds, or 5/16ths of a circle, which is equivalent to 112 degrees. The system of differently colored lights prescribed provides information to any observers that might otherwise be unseen because of the darkness of night.

All boats under 150 feet in length must show a white, 32-point light that can be seen for at least two miles while riding at anchor for the night. This light is known as the anchor light. Stern lights, and single bow lights, must also be white. Therefore, should you see only a white light on a boat ahead of you, you will immediately know that it is affixed to a boat that is either anchored for the night or that the boat is running in a forward direction ahead of you, heading in approximately the same direction as yourself. Should the boat to which this light is affixed be heading toward you, you would also see either a green light or a red light, or both. This is due to the fact that running lights are green and red ... red lights always being used on the boat's port side and green lights always being shown on the boat's starboard side. Each of these running lights must be set so as to cast a beam over an unbroken 10-point arc from dead ahead to two points behind the beam.

While lights are not specifically required by the rules to be used other than during the hours between sunset and sunrise, the law does not specifically prohibit their use during the hours between sunrise and sunset. The wise, safety-conscious boatman will always turn on his navigation lights during daylight hours when weather conditions cause reduction in normal visibility. Again, don't go strictly by the book when it comes to a matter of safety. Federal, as well as other governmental regulations, only set minimum standards.

NECESSARY EQUIPMENT

The previous section more or less detailed what the Coast Guard, in its stipulated regulations, calls for as minimum equipment which must be carried on board a boat. The law simply does not go far enough and any boatman going out on the water with only what is required by that law is going to find himself in (pardon the pun) a bit of hot water. For safety's sake, and for greater enjoyment of your boat and the time you spend on her, the following equipment is deemed to be necessary and should be purchased without hesitation. Some items in the next several pages are those which are needed in the usual, routine, every-day running of your boat; others will not be necessary until an emergency arises ... and then it may well be too late to go running to the nearest boat supply store.

TOOL KIT

The basic tool kit should include an adjustable end wrench (crescent), slip joint pliers, a pipe wrench, a vise grip, various sizes of screwdrivers, a box and wrench set, and a hammer. Also present in the kit should be a couple of spare spark plugs and, perhaps, some replacement engine parts, including a set of distributor points, a condenser, a coil, a fuel pump, and a spare fuel filter.

For marine use, specially manufactured tools of beryllium copper are available. The tools are spark and corrosion resistant, and non-magnetic. Tools of beryllium copper are considerably more expensive than the usual type but don't let the extra cost keep you from buying them. When needed, they are worth their weight in gold.

ROPE

There are three kinds of rope that may be purchased. The most widely used is Manila rope. It is low in cost, is long wearing, but it is not very strong. Rope made of polypropylene has about fifty percent more tensile strength than Manila rope. Polypropylene floats and is stronger wet than dry. It will not rot nor mildew. Polypropylene is used for mooring and towing lines. Nylon rope is twice as strong, and about twice as expensive, as Manila. Having an elastic characteristic, it is also suitable for anchor and mooring lines.

ANCHOR

Surprisingly enough, this is one of the items of necessary equipment which is not required by federal regulations or any other law. Yet, an anchor is essential if you want to stop the boat elsewhere than at a dock. Probably the most reliable motorboat anchor is one of the patent types, such as a Danforth or a Northill. They are light and collapsible. An eight-pound anchor is recommended for boats up to sixteen feet; for 16- to 20-footers a thirteen-pound anchor should be used; for all craft 20- to 40-feet in length, a 22-pounder is good.

FIRST-AID KIT AND MANUAL

There are many pre-packaged first-aid kits available on the market which are simply not adequate for marine use. The most complete kit possible should be purchased, and do not hesitate to consult your own family doctor regarding any item that might be added to the basic kit you buy. The kit should be stored in a watertight container and kept well beyond the reach of young children. One of the best and most comprehensive manuals is the one published by the American Red Cross. It is entitled *First Aid Textbook* and is available from any local chapter of the American Red Cross for a very nominal fee.

AUXILIARY POWER

What does one do when his small-sized motorboat cannot go because the motor has conked out? Well, there is one of two things you can do. If you are the type of boatman who has so much faith in his motor that you have not made provision for just such an emergency, you sit out in your boat and wait and pray for help to come your way. On the other hand, if you are a far-sighted, prudent skipper who hopes there will not be any such emergency but plans for one anyway, you will merely break out your telescoping oar, or paddle, and make for the shore. For use in small boats, these excellent items of equipment can be purchased at relatively little cost. Because the oar is in sections, it is easily stored. Of course, larger boats which are rigged with twin motors can limp back to port on one motor should one of the engines die. Carrying a spare motor is a needless expense, as the extra weight and space it would occupy makes it unsuitable for any but the largest craft. A spare motor should never be a substitute for proper or careful maintenance of the original.

COMPASS

A compass is an absolutely essential piece of equipment when navigating in unfamiliar water or when caught in poor visibility. Remember, should you get lost while on land you can always stop someone and ask directions so you can get to where you were going before you got lost; who are you going to ask when you get lost while afloat? Your compass may very well be your only source of possible help. So don't stint on this item. Get a good compass, one that is fitted with a water-tight cover, called a binnacle.

The primary purpose of the compass is to indicate to you the course your boat is on; it cannot tell you just where you are by itself.

SPARE FUEL AND TANK

Unless your boat is equipped with an optional fuel gauge, a drum of spare fuel would be well to take along. The drum must be air and water tight to prevent fumes from escaping and water from seeping in which would render the fuel useless. Come to think of it, taking a spare drum of fuel along is a good idea even if your engine *is* equipped with a fuel gauge. A lot of good your gauge will do if you run out of fuel.

BOAT HOOK

A boat hook is necessary for everything from fishing your hat or your pet out of the water to fending off the dock. For easy stowing, a telescoping model is best. The hook part should have a cork or rubber cap when not in use so that stupid accidents can be prevented.

BILGE PUMP

A small hand pump is good for little more than controlling a small leak and getting rid of rain water. Its effectiveness depends to a large extent on the strength and

stamina of the person operating it and it stops him from doing anything else that may require his attention. A small electric bilge pump, therefore, makes a good piece of equipment to have on board. It requires no work or attention while it is doing its job. A large, powerful bilge pump can keep a boat afloat even with a sizeable hole in its hull.

DETECTORS

There are detectors available to serve a variety of purposes. A gasoline fume detector will give a buzzing signal or a ringing sound or a whistle or turn on a flashing light when there are fumes at large. The signalling part of the detector can, and should, be installed so that it can easily be heard or seen by the "crew"; the connecting sensory part of the system is, of course, installed below. Other detecting systems can be installed aboard which will warn a skipper of water in the bilge, let the captain know when oil pressure has dropped below proper level, and other abnormal aspects aboard. Naturally, detecting systems should be considered only as supplementary to your own careful surveillance.

RADIO

Believe it or not, there is more on local radio stations than the latest in pop music. All during the day, these stations broadcast weather reports and during the boating season, a regular part of this report concerns itself with the marine weather forecast; including visibility and wind velocity. An

Radiotelephone: a valuable piece of communications equipment.

optional attachment that can be fitted onto radios is a direction finder. The finder will point toward the source of the radio transmission. This can be a valuable additional aid to navigation.

CHARTS

Charts are really road maps for use on water. They are inexpensive and continually revised. Charts include information such as water depths, mileage scales, bridge clearances, buoys, lighthouses, landmarks, sunken ships, plus a great deal more. These charts are published and sold by the United States Coast and Geodetic Survey, Washington Science Center, Rockville, Maryland. A free catalog is provided just for the asking. From the catalog, you can determine just which charts you will need.

BUCKET AND SPONGE

A clean boat is a tidy boat and that's as it should be. After all, your boat is nothing more than an extension of your home. Many boat owners take justifiable pride in their boat's appearance. A bucket, soap, sponge, mop, and polish do wonders to enhance the beauty of a boat and they are inexpensive and easily stored.

OPTIONAL EQUIPMENT

In this category are those pieces of equipment which are not required by law nor absolutely essential to the safe and efficient functioning of a boat. However, these are items which are "nice" to have if you can afford them and you would appreciate their added convenience.

METAL REFLECTORS

Metal reflectors are not listed among the necessary equipment because large metal craft do not need them. They are sheets of metal, sometimes collapsible, which will bounce back a radar signal. Dead in the water, a small boat may be overlooked and a wooden-hulled boat is incapable of bouncing back a signal. Metal reflectors are a good idea if your boat falls within either of these two categories.

BOARDING LADDER

A boarding ladder is a definite convenience if the boat is used for the purpose of swimming. Two-step ladders are inexpensive and hook over the transom at the stern of the boat. Three- and four-step ladders are more expensive and are used on cabin cruisers. It is much easier getting back into the boat from the water when a ladder is used.

WINDSHIELD WIPERS

While not too much boating is deliberately done in inclement weather, there is always the possibility of being caught by rain out on the water. Therefore, it is a good idea to have an efficient automatic electric windshield wiper installed. These are relatively inexpensive, with one of the lower-priced models going for something around $10.

SPOTLIGHT

Nighttime docking can be made a good deal easier by the use

of a spotlight. Also, a spotlight can be invaluable in locating objects which may fall into the water at night. Be sure to buy a good spotlight which is shock and corrosion resistant. The spotlight should be attached close to the helm so that it can easily be operated by the pilot.

FENDERS

The fenders used on modern-day pleasure boats are usually pieces of soft plastic threaded to a line attached to a deck cleat. Their function is to protect the hull from being damaged during the docking operation. There are somewhat expensive fenders which are made of air-filled rubber. Though costlier, they generally last longer.

GAUGES

It is always useful to know at what speed you are traveling. A speedometer gives the speed in miles per hour. A tachometer is also a mechanical means of measuring speed. However, this instrument records the speed of the motor in terms of revolutions per minute (rpm) and is an indication of how fast or how hard the motor is working. For example, to reach 35 mph quickly, you may run your motor up to 3,000 rpm. To maintain that speed once it has been achieved may require only 2,500 rpm. For long cruises, the motor should not be worked at a higher rpm than is absolutely necessary, as this makes it less efficient and is very wasteful as far as fuel consumption is concerned. A

middle range rpm is much more suitable. A gas gauge, indicating the amount of fuel remaining, has an obvious value.

TRAILERS

A trailer renders the boat portable, provided it is small enough to be carried on a trailer. With it, one can reach inland waters that are only accessible by car. Also, the boat can be transported from home to the ocean and back without the cost of a season-long dock rental.

Trailers are described in terms of their capacity. When purchasing a trailer, the weight and the length of the boat to be hauled should be known. Weight is the total weight of the boat, including the engine, fuel, and all the added equipment. If the total weight is within 100 pounds of the trailer capacity, then buy the next largest trailer, just to be completely on the safe side. To figure the length, measure the centerline from bow to stern. However, a boat with a pointed bow may require a shorter trailer than one of the same length which has a rounded bow.

The trailer should support the hull along most of its length. Equipment stowed within the boat must be securely fastened to prevent its movement and any subsequent damage to the boat.

The best trailer hitch is mounted to the body of the car. Except for very small boats, it is not a good idea to use a fender hitch. Also, for heavy loads, the trailer should have its own set of brakes. Some trailers have electrical brakes which are controlled from the inside of the car. Another type, requiring no manual labor, is the surge brake activator. As the car slows down, the trailer brakes are automatically applied. This type has the advantage that in a crucial situation, the driver has just to worry about stopping his car, without the added responsibility of braking the trailer. The trailer will brake itself.

The trailer must be equipped with tail and stop lights, as well as turn indicators. Also, the license plate must be mounted on the back of the trailer so that it is clearly visible.

SOUNDING DEVICE

Sounding devices are used to determine the depth of the water beneath a boat. While the primary purpose of knowing the depth of the water is to prevent the boat from being grounded in too-shallow water, a sounding device can also be an aid to navigation. As previously noted, navigational charts generally show water depths so that knowing the depth of the water can sometimes indicate your position. There are two types of sounding device. One is a simple line which has its length marked off at regular intervals by knots and to the end of which is attached a lead weight. The line is lowered overboard until the lead weight hits bottom. The depth is revealed by the number of knots which have gone overboard with the line. Slowly but surely coming into popular use is the other type of sounding device which is an electronic depth-finder. This one does all the work for you and is amazingly swift and accurate in giving its readings. The device sends out impulses which bounce off the bottom. The time it takes a signal to get to the bottom and back again is electronically and instantly measured and translated into the depth of the water in terms of feet. These sounding devices are quite handy in locating schools of passing fish if fishing is your purpose for being out in a boat.

Inadvertently overlooked in the section on *MANDATORY EQUIPMENT* was a legal requirement which is not really a piece of boating equipment at all. But nevertheless, it is required by law. That is the requirement that most all motorboats have to be registered with the Coast Guard and have a set of numbers identifying the craft issued. The numbers assigned to any specific boat have to be displayed on both sides of the boat, near the bow, in numerals at least three inches in height.

This registration has nothing at all to do with licensing. There are no tests that have to be taken nor any skills of boat handling or knowledge of marine law, etc. that have to be demonstrated. All that has to be done is that an application be filled out and sent along with the specified fee. In some instances, proof of ownership has to be shown.

Also, in the section on *NECESSARY EQUIPMENT,* there was an obvious oversight. No boat that is powered should ever leave its dock without a working *flashlight* and several spare *batteries.* •

CHAPTER SIX

Marine Insurance and Liability

■ It is a fact that insurance is not an item that one would be likely to consider part of a boat's equipment. Federal regulations do not require that insurance be carried as an item of mandatory equipment; it certainly isn't necessary insofar as proper running and maintenance of the boat is concerned; it won't make your time afloat any more enjoyable or comfortable as will items of optional equipment. However, should your boat ever be accidentally damaged or deliberately stolen, or should your boat ever accidentally damage somebody else's property, or should you or anyone on board your boat ever be hurt ... insurance could well be the most important piece of equipment you ever purchased. The wise boatman considers insurance every bit as much a part of his boat's equipment as his compass, radio or anchor.

True, the purchase of marine insurance is a gamble ... much the same sort of gamble that is involved in the purchase of any type of "If" insurance. "If" insurance is that type of protection which is purchased to ward off financial destruction *if* some unforeseen misfortune happens to strike. Included in this category are accident and health policies, household fire insurance policies, automobile insurance policies, etc. The purchaser of "if" insurance gambles that any loss or damage he incurs will result in greater financial loss than the cost of the premiums he must pay in order to be protected against the occurrence of such loss; the insuring company, or underwriter, gambles that the total amount of money it takes in as premiums will be greater than the total sum of money it must pay out as claims. The other category of insurance is "when" insurance and the only type of policy in that category is whole life insurance. This pays off *when* the insured dies and, being that no person ever born of woman has lived forever, there is never any question of *if,* only *when.* End of general insurance lesson and back to the specifics of marine insurance.

Premium rates for marine insurance are calculated pretty much on the same basis as premiums for automobile insurance . . . experience of loss suffered in any particular area, costs of replacement parts and repairs, value of the craft being insured, etc. As with automobile insurance, marine insurance premiums are relatively high. This is due, in large part, because of a small number of aquatic idiots who have never learned or do not care to learn how to handle their boat in a proper, safe manner. Nor do they abide by the simple code of water courtesy. These are the peabrained yo-yo's who are constantly smashing up their boats against docks or other boats, carelessly running the boats aground and damaging hulls, exploding, etc. These are the "boatmen" who are the primary reasons for seemingly exhorbitant marine insurance premium rates. This situation will undoubtedly improve as the public becomes more aware of the training and instruction available from the U.S. Power Squadrons

and the U.S. Coast Guard Auxiliary. It is also well within the realm of possibility that the day may come when people will have to take proficiency tests in order to obtain a boating license much as is done in order to obtain a license to drive an automobile. For the time being, about the only thing that a boat owner can do about keeping his insurance premium down to a reasonable rate is to buy only that insurance coverage which is suitable (but adequate) to his needs and to get proposals from at least two or three independent insurance agents who specialize in the field of marine insurance. Marine insurance rates are fairly negotiable and a marine insurance specialist can work to get you the best possible rate.

There are different types of marine insurance for different types of boats. Be sure that the type of insurance you buy best fits your particular situation.

INBOARDS, SAILBOATS, YACHTS

There are two types of coverage which protect inboard motorboats, sailboats, and large yachts (over 65 feet in length): (1) protection and indemnity, (2) hull insurance. The first coverage provides protection for losses suffered in personal injury and property damage accidents. Much the same as public liability and property damage coverages in automobile insurance, this coverage is available in a variety of limits . . . that is, limits for which the insurance company is liable. The second coverage provides protection against losses suffered due to damage through fire, vehicles, lightning, collision at sea, theft, explosion, malicious mischief, and a variety of other accidents which can happen during loading, unloading, and/or hauling out. The items on the boat specifically covered against the above perils are the hull, spars, sails, fittings, tackle, machinery, dinghy, other equipment and items of personal attire. The cost of this coverage is determined, to some extent, on the same basis as the comprehensive coverage portion of your automobile insurance. That is, the valuation of the boat, its age, and total replacement cost. In addition, consideration is given to the type of boat being insured . . . cruiser, runabouts, sloop, etc. . . . its overall length in ratio to its horsepower, what waters it will be used in, and whether or not there is to be included a deductible clause.

There are many factors to be on the watch for in buying this type of policy. These include a clause which may limit, or eliminate completely, the insurance company's liability for payments in the event of injury to persons or damage to property while your boat is being used for water skiing. Also, you may be required to pay an extra premium, called a surcharge, if you are to be using your boat for racing. Be very sure to check with your insurance agent whether or not your boat is covered by protection should you desire to charter or rent your boat in any way. Very often, insurance for privately-owned pleasure boats will only be in effect when the boat is used for the personal pleasure of the owner and his guests and the coverage is not extended to include the boat if it is rented out for a fee. Don't rely on yourself to read the policy . . . go over it carefully with the fellow who knows it best, your agent. Never be too ashamed to ask him to go over all the clauses, not just the major ones. Be especially attentive to all clauses which may be under the general heading of "Exclusions and Limits of Liability".

OUTBOARDS

Outboard motors and hull are covered by one of three general forms of insurance. The choice of which form to buy is strictly up to you and depends a great deal on how much you can afford in premiums and how much of the risk you can afford to assume yourself. In order of ascending cost (least expensive first), the forms of coverage are:

1—Limited Named Perils Insurance covers losses caused by fire, lightning, windstorm, transportation, and theft of motor or boat.

2—Broad Named Perils Insurance covers losses caused by fire, lightning, collision on both land and water, transportation, theft of motor or boat (or both) and a number of marine perils, including the loss of your motor by its falling into deep water.

3—All-Risk or Comprehensive Insurance covers the boat with protection against just about every conceivable contingency. That is why this is the most expensive form of coverage, costing approximately 4 per cent of the total value of the boat. The total value of the boat is computed as including the hull, the motor, and all equipment aboard.

All items of equipment generally are not covered by any one of the above forms of policy unless they are specifically mentioned in a "rider" to the basic policy, much the same as valuable items of personal jewelry, furs, photographic equipment, etc. must be listed separately in a homeowner's policy and a separate premium paid for their coverage. In marine insurance usage, "accessory items" mean those rather costly pieces of equipment such as life preservers, anchors, radios/radio-telephones, fishing tackle, etc.

None of the three forms of outboard insurance above insures the boatman against personal suit (loss) due to the injury of any person aboard his boat or to anyone injured by his boat. This type of insurance, which no prudent boat owner will be without, must be attached to the physical (boat)-loss policy in the form of a rider.

Should you be the proud owner of an outboard motor rated at more than 10 hp, be sure your insurance agent is made aware of it so you can be charged for a high-powered motor in your liability insurance. Do not attempt to hide this fact in order to save a few dollars. Failure to inform the company and pay the extra premium can leave you stripped of all liability coverage. There is not enough anti-acid in the world to quell the upset in your stomach should you seriously damage or destroy another man's boat, especially a really expensive one, and find that you had saved a few dollars in premium earlier in the year only to be naked, insurance-wise, at the very moment you needed coverage the most. What we are really trying to tell you is . . . don't ever make any false or misleading statements on an insurance application form. It just isn't worth the few dollars you may wind up saving. You could wind up having your policy voided or by having your application for renewal denied. And should you ever have your policy cancelled because of false statements, careless boat operation, or frequent accidents and ensuing claims, you may find it difficult to obtain insurance from another company. Insurance companies have a habit of exchanging bits of information about their policyholders . . . especially those they have cancelled or to whom renewal has been denied.

To sum up, be good to yourself and everybody who will ever be your guest on board your boat by carrying a sufficient amount of insurance coverage of a suitable type for your needs. Consult your insurance broker; he is probably the best source of information as to how much coverage and what type of coverage you should purchase. Most brokers will sell you the coverage that you need and no more . . . they will not load you up with coverage you don't need for the sake of earning a few dollars more in commissions.

Remember, you will never miss not having insurance . . . until you need it. ●

CHAPTER SEVEN

Fueling Your Boat

■ Whenever a motorboat is being loaded with fuel (it just won't go anywhere without fuel in its tank), there is always the possibility that there will be gasoline vapors in the immediate vicinity. Therefore, fueling the boat must be considered one of the most serious pieces of business conducted around the boat. It is a task that must be performed in a most careful, methodical manner. Unfortunately, there are times when it is done carelessly and thoughtlessly. And, this often leads to dangerous and sometimes tragic situations. Gasoline vapors are extraordinarily flammable at the very least. Should there occur a heavy-enough concentration of them, they become highly volatile and can explode at any moment should there be the slightest spark anywhere near them. There can never be too much care exercised in the fueling of a boat. Conduct this operation as though your very life depended on its proper execu-

tion . . . it may well be.

The following is presented as a checklist and should be stringently adhered to each and every time you add fuel to your boat's tank.

BEFORE FUELING

1—Make absolutely certain that every individual in the general vicinity of the boat which is being fueled thoroughly douses all cigarettes, cigars, and pipes. Be sure to caution all passengers and anyone else in the area to refrain from smoking or using matches or lighters. Not until after the fueling operation has been totally completed, and enough time has elapsed to permit all vapors to vanish, may smoking be resumed.

2—Make absolutely certain that every piece of electrical equipment aboard or nearby that has the capacity of producing a spark has its power turned off. Don't overlook the galley, if there is one on board your boat. This warning applies to anyone working in the close vicinity with an acetyline torch or someone in the galley making a pot of coffee. Gasoline fumes and/or vapors have a way of finding their way to open flames and must be guarded against in any and all instances.

3—All hatches, doors, and windows should be closed before starting to pour fuel into your boat's tank. Gasoline fumes are heavier in weight than air and have the capability of collecting in the very lowest recesses of the boat. All entrance ways to areas below deck must be tightly shut so that this is prevented from happening.

4—Completely check and re-check all the mooring lines until you are absolutely positive that the boat is held fast to the dock, without any risk of the boat moving. Should the mooring lines have any slack or play in them, the boat may drift during the fueling procedure. If that were permitted to happen, it is quite possible that the gasoline nozzle would work its way free of the engine intake pipe, causing volatile fuel to spill all over the boat.

5—A fire extinguisher should be kept in readiness, within easy reach, just in case anything should go wrong despite all the above precautions. The most portable type of extinguisher is one containing carbon dioxide. This type of fire extinguisher will snuff out a fire, should one somehow start, and will leave no messy residue to clean up afterwards. Be sure to ascertain that the fire extinguisher's contents are under the proper amount of pressure.

WHILE FUELING

1—As you start the fueling operation, do not be hesitant about reminding everyone in the vicinity to refrain from smoking or doing anything else that might result in a spark being present.

2—Make metal-to-metal contact by placing the fuel nozzle against the fill pipe of the fuel tank. Due to the fact that the motor is properly grounded, placing the fuel nozzle against the fill pipe will cause it too to be grounded. This will go a long way to help prevent the formation of a static spark which, in turn, could very easily ignite the fuel being loaded aboard.

3—Be especially careful to avoid the spilling of any fuel. Most spillage takes place when the fuel tank is already full and more fuel is added. This excess spills over onto the deck and presents a clearly dangerous situation. The best way of avoiding this happening is to know exactly how much fuel is needed to fill the tank and then pump in just a little less than that amount. Gasoline has a habit of expanding, especially in warm weather, and it is more economical, and safer, to put a little less gasoline in the tank than is indicated by the gauge.

AFTER FUELING

1—Break the good news to everyone around that they can soon resume smoking but that they shouldn't do it just yet. There are several further precautions to be taken first.

2—In the event there has been

an inadvertant spillage of fuel onto the deck, wipe up all the excess. Better still, hose down the deck.

3—Get rid of any gasoline or oil-soaked rags that have been used by disposing of them on shore. Do not leave them aboard the boat.

4—Open all the hatches, doors, and windows that had been closed to aid in ventilating the boat after fueling. In case there are any lingering fumes, this ventilating of the boat will help to dispel them. Permit the air to circulate throughout the boat for a minimum of five minutes.

5—Carefully go over the boat, checking for fumes. Do not depend solely on any fume-detecting devices you may have on board. There is no better fume-detecting mechanism than the sensitive sense of smell nature has installed in your nostrils. Sniff around the outside of the boat, as well as around the motor and fuel lines. If yours is a boat that is powered by an inboard engine, turn on the blowers to clear out any fumes you may have missed.

Only after you are completely and positively convinced that there are no lingering gasoline fumes present should you permit the resumption of normal activities, such as smoking and making coffee, etc. Then, and only then, can you feel safe enough to start up the engine and prepare to take off on your boating trip.

It is most important that the fuel system be maintained in complete accordance to the manufacturer's recommendations. Prudent boating procedure dictates that the fuel system, as well as all other working mechanisms and safety equipment aboard, be inspected periodically to make sure it is functioning properly. It is amazing what a well-trained eye can tell at a glance. For example, if the fuel line fittings feel damp, it generally means the gasoline is escaping and evaporating. Not only is this wasteful, it is also a bit dangerous. Regularly scheduled inspections will pick up many minor discrepancies before they turn into major problems. You have your family automobile checked over periodically, don't you? Why not do the same for the boat?

BUYING GASOLINE FOR YOUR BOAT

There is very litte, if any, difference in quality or octane rating between gasoline sold for marine use and gasoline sold for automobile use. However, marine gasoline is priced a few cents a gallon higher than gasoline sold along the highway. Why? Well, a sense of the practical says that this is in no small way due to the fact that the sale of marine gasoline is a seasonable business so per day profits have to be somewhat larger. Also, truckers may find it a little more difficult to approach the fueling station storage tanks on the water's edge. If you are aware of this and want to save a few cents on your boat's fuel bill, buy some good, sturdy metal carrying cans and have them filled at a highway gas station on your way to your boat. Just bear in mind, though, that gasoline weighs about six pounds per gallon. ●

CHAPTER EIGHT

How To Handle A Boat

■ In beginning to study the principles of how to handle a boat, it is important to understand just *why* a boat behaves as she does when you are out on the water handling her. Understanding the reasons for her behavior, should she turn one way when you really wanted her to turn the other, will result in your being less likely to repeat whatever mistake you may have made the first time.

There are basically three types of motor-powered boats: single-screw inboard, twin-screw inboard, and outboard (which includes the sterndrive or, as it is sometimes called, inboard-outboard). The first two of these types make use of a rudder or rudders which work in conjunction with a constant direction of thrust from the boat's propeller or propellers, as the case may be. Outboards are steered by directed thrust only, not having any rudder.

It is true that there are a great many people who have learned to handle a boat with great skill who have never read a page in any book on the subject of seamanship. They have done all of their learning in the tough school of experience ... and many have graduated with honors. Many of these people, however, have grown up in the environment of commercial fishing and have been trained in the proper method of handling a boat practically from infancy. Not too many of us are raised in this manner nor would we want to be. Therefore, it behooves us to learn all we can about the principles of handling the average boat under conditions which can be considered normal and then supplement this acquired knowledge with actual experience aboard our own boat and as many different boats as we can get to run. Nothing in the whole wide world is an adequate substitution for the experience gained in actually handling boats and it is essential that you get all the experience that time and money permit. The reason for gaining experience in handling other boats beside your own is that no two boats behave in exactly the same manner under every situation. Each boat has its own peculiar individuality and eccentricity. There are many factors which affect a boat's performance, including the design of the boat, its hull's underbody, the basic construction of the boat, the shape and position of its rudder as well as the area covered by the rudder, the boat's trim, speed, weight, load, etc. Beside gaining book knowledge and actual boat handling experience, develop your boat sense still further by carefully observing experienced yachtsmen, fishermen, and Coast Guardsmen when they are in the act of handling their craft.

In these pages, we are not going to attempt to go into the complete details of the steps in docking, anchoring, leaving the dock or mooring, and other elements of good boat handling. We are much too limited in form and size to accomplish all of that. What we intend to do is give you the basic information regarding the safe handling of a boat. For further and far more detailed study, we strongly recommend that you avail yourself of a copy of *Piloting, Seamanship and Small Boat Handling,* written by Charles F. Chapman and published by The Hearst Corporation.

BASIC PRINCIPLES

Before going into the actual handling of a boat in specific situations, let's dwell a bit on how a boat makes its turns. Most of us own and drive automobiles and we know that the front wheels of the car determine the direction in which the car will be traveling, whether we are going forward or in reverse. By means of the car's steering wheel, we turn the wheels at the front end of the car . . . to the right if we want to make a right forward turn, to the left if we want to make a left forward turn. When going in reverse, turning the front wheels to the right will cause the front of the car to go to the left while the rear of the car goes to the right; just the opposite will occur when the steering wheel is turned to the left. In any event, it is the *front* of the car which determines direction. Unlike the controlling action of the automobile, the steering of a boat is controlled by its stern, or *rear* of the boat. This is because the rudder, which is the peice of mechanism that controls the direction in which the boat will go (much like the front wheels of your car) is in the stern end of the boat. Or rather, in back of the stern end.

THE ACTION OF THE RUDDER

Motor boats have steering gears that are almost always rigged so that they turn in conjunction with the rudder (this applies only to inboard powered boats as, as mentioned earlier, outboards do not have rudders). In other words, when the wheel, or rather the top of the wheel, is turned to port (left), the rudder is thrown also to port. Therefore, when the boat is going forward (having headway), turning the wheel to port will give the boat left rudder which will cause the stern to go to starboard (the right). In this manner, the bow (front of the boat), will turn to the left. On the other hand, if the top of the wheel is turned to starboard, the rudder goes to the right and the stern is kicked around toward the left, causing the boat to turn to the right. When going in reverse, the action of the wheel and the rudder remain exactly the same. The only thing that changes is the direction in which the boat will go. That is, when the wheel is turned to port, the boat will be given left rudder and the boat, being in reverse (having sternway) will cause the stern of the boat to kick toward the left and it will move in that direction. In this respect, the action is that of an automobile being driven in reverse.

PROPELLERS

Depending on the direction in which they rotate, propellers are either right-handed or left-handed. The way to find out whether your boat has a right- or left-handed propeller, is to stand outside your boat and look at its stern, or aft of the propeller. Look toward the driving face of the propeller as it starts to rotate. If the top of the

Always use the proper-size propeller.

propeller goes toward your right (clockwise) when the boat is being driven in a forward direction, it is a right-handed propeller; if the top goes toward the left (counterclockwise), it is a left-handed propeller. This is an important factor in the maneuvering of a boat. However, as most propellers are of the right-handed variety, we will assume that the one on your boat is of that type.

It is actually the propeller which causes the boat to move through the water. The action of a propeller is very much like that of a pump. It draws in water (when going forward) from in front of the boat and throws it out astern of the boat. This forced stream of water pushes against the water around it and propels the boat forward. The reverse action of the propeller and the water it controls makes the boat go backward.

When a boat is powered by an outboard motor, the action of the propeller is the same as outlined above. However, the positioning of the propeller in the water, as determined by the helmsman,

controls the direction in which the boat travels. In other words, the propeller fills the function of both propelling and steering mechanism.

SPECIFICS OF BOAT HANDLING

As previously mentioned, most inboards have right-handed propellers which rotate clockwise when viewed from astern. Because of this, the stern has a natural tendency to swing momentarily to the left. Therefore, it is a good idea, whenever possible, to circle to the right when making a complete U-turn. This will take advantage of the natural inclination of the stern, which makes for an easier right turn.

Learning to handle a boat properly takes a knowledge of the basic principles involved and a great deal of practice. With the experience gained by applying the basic principles to actually handling a boat in the water, the task is mastered fairly easily. After all, many thousands have already done so, among them being a great number of very young people. Under no circumstances should you become discouraged if, at first, you feel awkward and your maneuvers seem to be jerky and possibly even a bit nerve-wracking to those on board with you. After all, nobody ever just got in behind the wheel of a car for the first time and became a model driver. It takes a knowledge of the elements controlling the behavior of a boat and a good deal of boating experience to acquire the polish or *finesse* needed to run a boat like an old salt. Just keep in mind the two most important things you should do, especially when learning how to handle a boat: move slowly (so you will always leave yourself time enough to react to situations which may arise) and, just as you do when driving your automobile, always look where you are going.

LEAVING THE DOCK

There are two methods used for launching a boat which is docked alongside a pier or wharf. Which method to use depends solely on whether the dock is crowded or not crowded (open).

LAUNCHING FROM AN OPEN DOCK

1—Carefully cast-off all lines. Double-check to make sure that there are no mooring lines which hold the boat secured to the dock. This is a most important point.

2—Turn the wheel of your inboard, or your outboard, very slightly in the direction away from the dock. Should you make the mistake of turning the wheel too far in the direction of open water, you will surely cause the stern to swing into the dock with possible resultant damage. The initial direction taken should be just a shade off a straight forward one.

3—Once you have moved in this slightly angled direction sufficiently so that the boat is anywhere from one to two hull lengths from the dock, turn toward the open water. You have now allowed the stern enough room to swing about freely, with no danger of hitting anything.

LAUNCHING FROM A CROWDED DOCK

1—As when launching from an open dock, cast-off all lines, *except the bow line.* Leave the bow line securely tied to its mooring. Doing this will cause the boat to pivot around the bow, which is just what you want it to do.

2—Put the boat in forward gear very, very slowly, barely moving in a forward direction. As the boat pivots on its bow, the stern will turn away from the dock and will present itself toward the open water.

3—When this has been accomplished, put the motor in neutral and cast off the bow line. Your boat is now lined up so that you can safely move it out into the open water.

4—Center the wheel or outboard and put the motor into its reverse gear. This will enable the boat to back out into open water. When you have completely cleared the dock, and it is completely safe to do so, change back to forward gear and take off on your cruise.

LEAVING A MOORING

Many marinas provide a mooring at which to keep your boat while it is in the water. This means that you leave your boat at anchor, usually a few hundred feet offshore. The anchor, which is supplied by the marina, is generally of the type known as a "mushroom anchor" because it resembles an inverted specimen of the vegetable after which it is named. The location of the anchor is marked by a small buoy.

The buoy also serves the purpose of keeping the anchor line afloat on the surface so you can find it and grab it easily when coming in for the day (or night). If your boat is one of those which are moored in this manner, you get out to it from shore either in a dinghy (which you will trail behind you while you go cruising) or a motor launch belonging to and operated by the marina. Unless you are a member of a yacht club, you will probably go out in a dinghy.

It is a bit simpler getting away from a mooring than it is from a dock. But there is a both a right way and a wrong way to do it. By doing it the wrong way, you incur the risk of having either the mooring line or the dinghy painter (the line which holds the dinghy secured to your boat while cruising) get fouled in your boat's propeller.

Assuming that a dinghy was used in reaching the boat, shorten up its painter as much as possible so that the reversing action of the propeller won't pull any slack down onto itself. Make sure that any and all boarding ladders, fenders and boat booms are in the boat. Then send one of your "crew" forward to let the mooring line go while you pilot the boat. In any body of water where there is a current, the boat will move away from the mooring as soon as the mooring line is released. In a very short period of elapsed time, the mooring line will cease to be of any concern. However, should you be in a body of water where there is no current or wind present to move the boat

when you have let go of the mooring line, you must be careful. If you were to go forward, the odds are all in favor of fouling the propeller with the mooring line. This would be the wrong way.

The right way is to go in reverse a few lengths of the boat. Go far enough so that you can keep the buoy in sight and give yourself enough room so that you can clear it when you go forward. There should be sufficient room to allow for the swinging of your stern as you pass the buoy. When backing away from the mooring, do it slowly and either in a straight backward line or in a slight turn. The direction depends solely on the proximity and location of other boats in the anchorage area. Run the motor fairly well throttled down until you are completely clear of the anchorage. Otherwise, you would be creating a nuisance to other boats with your wake. All this while, you have kept the dinghy's painter shortened. Once you've opened up to cruising speed, you can drop the dinghy back to a position where it is near the crest of the second wave to your rear. If you allow the dinghy to go back beyond that second crest, she will prove difficult to tow as she will continually be running uphill, her bow high in the air. The painter's length should be such that the dinghy runs fairly flat, at a good trim.

ANCHORS AND ANCHORING

There are a number of different types of anchors. Of these, three are best suited to serve the needs of powered boats. The *yachtsman's* anchor, as one might easily suspect, is large and quite heavy. This makes it appropriate mainly for boats considered really big, those over 65 feet in length. This anchor gives its best performance in waters that are sheltered and slow. The *mushroom* anchor is mostly used as a temporary hold for small fishing boats, and, as indicated before, is also used by many marinas as moorings. It is also quite effective as a permanent anchor for docking over soft, mudlike bottoms. The most popular anchors currently in use are the *patent* models. There are two of these . . . the Danforth and the Northill anchors. Both of them are light and collapsible for easy storage aboard. And once they have dug in to the bottom, both of them have good holding power.

The line that connects an anchor with a vessel is called the *anchor rode.* The length of the rode is referred to in terms of *scope.* The greater the scope, the more effectively the anchor will hold to the bottom. A judgment must be made of the current and wind strength before deciding on the best scope. Under normal conditions, a scope three times longer than the bottom depth is sufficient. Should there be extreme wind or current present, a scope ten times the bottom depth is recommended.

The process of dropping and securing the anchor is one facet of seamanship which is quite easily mastered. First, head directly into the wind or current and shift the motor's gears into neutral. As the boat comes to a stop, carefully and slowly let out the rode until it goes slack. The rode going slack indicates that the anchor has touched bottom. If the rode is marked off, make a notation of the water depth. You should never toss an anchor from a boat (as is at times done in the movies). You run the risk of fouling the line. To set the anchor so that it will serve its function of holding the boat fast within a prescribed radius, reverse the motor so that the boat moves backward gently until it is felt that the flukes (the part of the anchor that imbeds itself) are dug in and holding firmly.

BEACHING

Because the motor can be raised out of harm's way, an outboard can be brought directly into the shore for camping or picnicking. Never even consider beaching an inboard, though.

Choose a spot which appears to have a soft, rock-free bottom (although the outboard can be raised out of harm's way, a bottom which is made up of sharp rocks or other projections could easily damage the hull). Raise the outboard until the propeller is just barely beneath the waterline and with full power, send the bow onto the beach. If necessary, raise the outboard completely out of the water just before contact is made with the beach. To beach the craft securely, jump out of the boat and manually haul the bow onto the beach.

It is strongly recommended that, if at all possible, attach the bow line to a nearby tree or to a tent peg driven well into the sand,

Raise the outboard completely out of the water before beaching your boat.

to prevent the boat from slipping back into the water and away from you. If you know you have beached your boat in waters that are subject to incoming and ebbing tides, secure the boat's anchor well off the stern. Should the tide go out, leaving your boat high and dry on the beach, you'll be glad to take this rather simple precaution. Because then you'll be able to haul the hull into the water by

kedging, or pulling the boat toward the anchor by means of the rode.

TOWING

The length of the tow line is the most important factor in successful towing. Of course, the tow line should be strong enough to take the stress placed on it by the act of towing.

One end of the line should be tied to a stern cleat on the towing vessel and the other end should be fastened low onto the bow of the boat being towed. Small, light boats are efficiently towed if they ride just back of the second wake. Heavy boats are more suitably towed if they ride just forward of the top of either the first or the second wake.

DOCKING

Being able to properly dock a boat requires a great amount of experience which comes only after a great amount of practice. So do not become discouraged if it is done in a somewhat sloppy manner the first few times.

When approaching the dock, move slowly. Go just fast enough to maintain control of the boat. You may find it best to bring the boat to a complete stop while you are still a few boat lengths from the dock and then proceed by alternately putting the motor in forward and neutral.

Depending on the current and/or wind direction, there are several ways of approaching the docking area. Never head into the current or wind as they will have a tendency to either push the boat past the dock or else directly into it. Be sure the boat's fenders are attached.

If wind and current are not a factor, the usual method is to approach the dock at about a 30 degree angle. Turn the wheel or outboard very slowly until the boat is parallel to the docking area. Then reverse gears to instantly stop the boat and proceed to secure the lines.

If the wind and current are from the leeward side (wind off the dock), then approach the dock at a sharp angle until the bow of the boat makes contact, and secure the bow line. (Again, this entire procedure is done at very slow speed.) Next, turn the wheel or outboard away from the dock, put the motor in forward gear, and the stern will swing into the dock. Then secure all lines.

When approaching the docking area from the weather side (wind toward the dock), halt the boat a few feet aft and parallel to the berth. The boat will simply drift into the dock. Then secure all lines.

DECK LINES

A small boat needs only three different types of deck lines for safe mooring. They are the bow line, the stern line, and a set of spring lines.

The bow and stern lines are used for securing the fore and aft to the dock. In most docking situations in which the boat is tied up for short periods, or where there is quiet water, only the bow and stern lines are necessary. Just in case, however, the bow and stern lines should be fastened to the dock using a bowline knot.

The spring lines prevent fore and aft movement of the boat when tied to the dock. They fit over the bow or stern cleat and, respectively, run aft or forward to the dock cleat. They should be quite long. A spring line about as long as the boat itself is ample enough for any situation. The most secure manner of tying a boat is to use both port and starboard spring lines, as well as the bow and stern lines. If the docking area is subject to tides, the spring lines should be slack to allow for the rise and fall of the boat.

KNOTS

To securely fasten the boat to the dock or to the anchor, a knowledge of knots is necessary. Five basic types are sufficient for just about every tying need.

1—The bowline knot is used for making a permanent loop which can be slipped over a pier piling. The knot is made by making a loop (bite), then bringing the free end back through the loop, around the line, and back through the loop again.

2—One of the easiest knots to make for securing a line to a piling is the half hitch. Drape the line around the piling. Bring the free end over and under the long end and then over and under itself and through the loop.

3—The clove hitch is a quickly made knot used to attach a line temporarily to a dock piling. A second loop is made with the free end and also placed over the piling. When a clove hitch is strained, it tends to tighten, making it hard to free.

4—A square knot is used for tying together two ends. Loop one line and then bring the second up through and under.

5—The fisherman's bend is an excellent knot for attaching a line to a buoy or anchor. Loop the line twice around the eyelet. Bring the free end across the line, through the loop, and then again around the line. ●

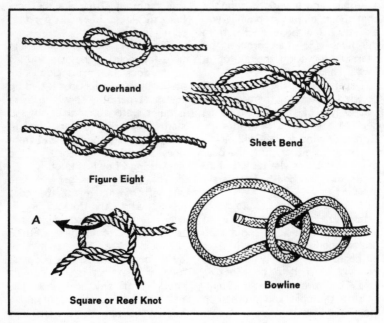

Overhand

Sheet Bend

Figure Eight

A

Square or Reef Knot

Bowline

CHAPTER NINE

Responding
To Situations

■ Proper handling of a boat calls for much more than simply learning how to leave a dock or mooring and return, just the same as there is much more to driving an automobile than just pulling away from a curb and parking. Once you're out on the open highway or on a city street, there are going to be situations arising which call for speedy responses. The same situations exist and arise on the open waters. Some of the situations that you will come across while out enjoying a day on the water will call for common-sense responses; others will call for responses which are dictated by legal rules and regulations. Just as there are highway safety driving laws, so, too, are there watery road safety boating laws. Sometimes the common-sense and legal responses called for are exactly the same; at other times, the only way to avoid an accident is to follow the rules exactly as they are promulgated. This comes about most often when it seems almost as wise to use one means of response to a sticky situation as it would be to use another. In situations such as these, where boatmen might have a choice of action and that choice might likely lead to a collision, legislators have taken the choice out of the hands of the boatmen and have decided for them exactly how they are to respond. By doing so, they have taken a great deal of possible confusion out of boating on the highways of the sea. By setting down rules of driving behaviour which must be adhered to by all boatmen in specific situations, they have made all boat-

men's reactions predictable and have, thereby, made it far more safe to be afloat. In general terms, the regulations set down by the federal government in the United States are known as . . .

RULES OF THE ROAD

There are actually four somewhat differing sets of rules which go to make up the Rules of the Road. These are regional rules, each-governing a separate waterway or system of waterways: Great Lakes (rules for these can be found in Coast Guard pamphlet CG-172); Western Rivers (for which the rules can be found in Coast Guard pamphlet CG-184); Inland, and International, waterways (the official rules for both of which can be found in Coast Guard pamphlet CG-169). Most operators of pleasure boats are affected by the Rules of the Road concerning inland waterways. For that reason, and also because all the sets of rules are basically similar to each other, we are going to concentrate on the Inland Rules.

RIGHT-OF-WAY

When driving along urban streets or rural highways in our family car, we are governed, to a great extent, by traffic lights, stop signals, and other similar official indicators which dictate which automobile has the right-of-way when meeting at intersections or crossroads. Also, most streets and highways are clearly laid out in specific lanes which traffic follows when going in a forward direction. However, there are no traffic

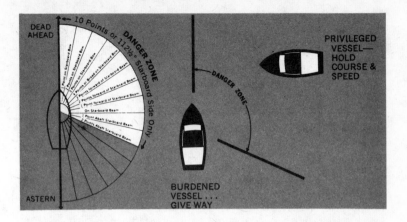

Boat having right-of-way is "privileged vessel." Other craft is "burdened vessel."

lights or stop signals or clearly defined traffic lanes on the broad expanse known as the watery road. It is, therefore, of extreme importance that each and every boat pilot (driver) learn and adhere to the common rules of the road. If at any time you are unsure of what to do in any particular situation, bear in mind that above all else, safety and courtesy come first. Rather than make any unsafe moves when you are not absolutely certain as to what to do, come to a complete stop and let the other boat move on. Never be bull-headed and try to argue the point of who has the right-of-way and who doesn't. The worst that can happen by following this logical and common-sense procedure is that you are putting yourself in the position of losing a few minutes of time . . . and when out pleasure boating, time should not be so important a consideration that you would risk having a possibly serious accident. Far more time would be lost should

that happen, so be smart.

Discussion of right-of-way infers that two boats are approaching an area where, unless one boat permits the other to continue without hinderance, there exists the possibility of an accident taking place. In boating terminology, the boat which has the right-of-way according to prescribed rules is the *privileged* vessel. This means that this boat continues on its course. The craft which must either veer off or slow down or come to a complete stop in order to offer no hindrance to the privileged boat is known as the *burdened* vessel.

As noted in Chapter Five, *Equipment,* one of the items of mandatory equipment was a whistle, as well as other signalling devices. In the matter of following the rules of the road, these devices are used to inform the operators of each of the boats involved in certain encounters what the intentions are of the signalling boat and that the boat being signalled has heard and understood the signal. This will be explained in more specific detail further on in this chapter.

Throughout this chapter, we will be discussing the rules as they apply to power-driven vessels. Boats which are propelled by both motors and sails are considered power-driven and must adhere to these rules the same as pure motorboats. Boats that are completely without power machinery, such as pure sailboats or boats propelled by oars, are always the privileged vessels when encountering power-driven boats. Because they are without power, they are less maneuverable than motorboats and can be severely hampered by the wake created by a speeding motorboat. Therefore, non-motorboats always have the right-of-way with respect to power-driven craft. Of course, as with so many of our absolute rules, there are exceptions. In the unlikely but still possible event that a non-motor driven craft overtakes a motorboat, the sail boat (assuming that this is the case) becomes the burdened vessel and must abide by all the rules that address themselves to overtaking situations. Also, her normal privileged status does not give a sailboat the right to hamper the progress of a power-driven boat in a narrow channel if the power-driven boat can only navigate safely within the limits of the channel. In an encounter with vessels which are engaged in fishing, a sailing vessel is likewise not the priviledged vessel.

As stated earlier, discussion of right-of-way infers that there is a situation where two vessels are about to become involved in an encounter. There are actually three types of encounters possible: meeting, crossing, and overtaking. All three can be generally classed as *passing* situations. However, we will discuss the right-of-way rules as they apply to each of the three separate situations.

WHEN MEETING

A meeting situation exists when two power-driven vessels approach one another either head on, or nearly so. Article 18, Rule 1 of the Inland Rules declares that it is the duty of each of the vessels to pass on the port side of the other vessel. Neither of these boats actually has the right-of-way over the other and both, if necessary, must move to starboard (the right) to allow sufficient room for safe passage. This should be an easy rule to remember as all automobile drivers live by the rule of keeping to the right in the event you meet an oncoming car on a narrow road.

In order for this rule covering a meeting situation to be applicable, there are two basic requirements that must be met. One, the meeting is being accomplished in such a manner that there is definite risk

Meeting head-on, turn to starboard.

MEETING HEAD-ON

of collision involved. Two, the two boats must be facing each other end on to end or very nearly so. This means that, during daylight hours, the masts of one boat is either on line, or nearly lined up with, the masts of the other boat. If this encounter occurs at night, each must be able to cearly see both sidelights of the other. In other words, the risk of collision must be clearly defined. This rule of passing on the other's port or moving to starboard to achieve this does not apply at all if the two vessels are far enough to the side of each other so that, without altering course or speed, they will be able to pass clear of each other.

Article 18, Rule 1 prescribes that when two vessels do meet in a normal meeting situation, the first boat to recognize that a meeting situation exists must give a definite signal of her intention to pass the other port-to-port. The prescribed signal consists of one short and definite blast of the boat's whistle (more often than not a horn is actually used and is perfectly permissible under the meaning of the rule). If the signal is understood by the skipper of the other boat, he replies immediately with the same signal. However, should the other boat's pilot believe that to pass in this manner is dangerous or should he be in doubt regarding the situation, he must respond with the danger signal. The danger signal consists of four or more short blasts in rapid succession. The rules do not specify which boat in a meeting situation must signal first ... both boats are on an equal level with neither having clearly defined

right-of-way and so, either can make the first signal to the other.

When the approaching vessels are so far to the side of each other that the rule for passing does not apply and the boats will be passing to starboard of each other, rather than port-to-port, the whistle signal to be given and answered is two short, clear blasts. Under no circumstances is a one-blast signal to be answered by a two-blast or a two-blast signal to be answered by a one-blast reply. This is known as *cross signals* and is strictly prohibited as the ensuing confusion on the part of either of the boat skippers could result in the collision neither of them wants.

Should the normal passing signal of one boat be replied to by the sounding of the danger signal by the other boat, both boats must immediately slow down to a mere crawl or come to a dead stop until there is agreement between them as to what is about to be done. This agreement is demonstrated by an exchange of similar signals. Under no circumstances should either boat try to pass the other until there is this exchange of similar signals.

WHEN CROSSING

When two boats approach each other at right angles, and it is obvious that there is risk of collision unless one or the other changes course, the rules state that the boat on the other's starboard (right) side has the right-of-way. This is exactly the same rule that applies to two automobiles approaching an uncontrolled (by signals or signs) intersection. This

Rule of the Road clearly defines a boat's "danger zone" (*dee zee*). This zone is the form of an arc which reaches from almost dead ahead to a point that is two nautical points abaft the starboard beam. Anytime you see another boat within this danger zone, you are to give this boat the right-of-way. She is the privileged vessel and yours is the burdened vessel. You must keep out of her way by so directing, or altering your heading, that you will cross the other's path at her stern (in back of her) rather than ahead of her. You must come to a dead stop, slacken your speed, change your course, or go into reverse, if necessary. On the other hand, the vessel which is privileged *must* maintain her heading and speed totally unaltered. While whistle signals are not specifically required by the Inland Rules in a crossing situation, the privileged vessel is permitted to sound one short blast as a signal indicating her recognition of her role as the privileged vessel and that she will continue to proceed on course at the same speed. Though not required, it is wise and safer for the privileged vessel to do this. Also, while not required to do so, it would be most prudent and courteous for the burdened vessel to reply in kind to indicate that there is complete understanding of the situation. Should there be any reason why either vessel can't adhere to the rules of right-of-way as prescribed in a crossing situation, the vessel so encumbered must sound the danger signal. When this happens, both vessels must come to a complete stop and even back up, if necessary, until such time that signals for safe passing of each other have been made and replied to by the other. Then, and only then, can each vessel proceed.

As previously stated regarding the rules regarding meeting situations, the rules covering crossing situations do not apply if there is clearly no risk of collision. When it is obvious that the vessels in question will pass each other by very safe distances, neither one of them is privileged or burdened. However, if there is the slightest question on the part of either skipper, the Rules of the Road should be adhered to and whistle signals should be exchanged to make sure that the intentions of one boat are clearly understood by the other.

WHEN OVERTAKING

Whenever two boats are following a similar heading and one boat is to the rear (astern) of the other and the rearward boat is going faster than the forward boat, an overtaking situation is certainly in the making. In each and every instance of this type, the rearward boat, which is doing the overtaking, is the burdened boat; the boat being overtaken is the privileged vessel. In no way whatsoever is the burdened boat permitted to hinder the progress of the privileged boat.

There is a prescribed system of signalling which must be used by the burdened (overtaking) boat before she is permitted to pass the privileged (overtaken) boat. If the boat which is astern desires to pass on the port side of the boat being overtaken (the normal rule

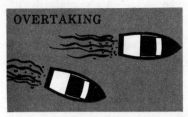

OVERTAKING

Rear vessel "burdened" when overtaking.

of any road, concrete or water, is keep to the right and pass to the left), she must signal by sounding off with two short blasts of her whistle or horn. In the event the privileged boat has no reason to reject this passing, she replies with two short blasts of her own. This signal should be given immediately as an indication of understanding of, and agreement to, the signal of the burdened boat. The speedier, overtaking boat can then proceed to alter its course slightly to port and proceed with the passing operation. If, for one reason or another, the overtaking boat wishes to pass the slower boat to starboard (not usual but perfectly legal), it must give one short blast of its whistle as a signal of its intentions. If this maneuver is agreeable to the boat being overtaken, it replies with a similar blast of its whistle. The speedier boat then proceeds to alter its course slightly to starboard and passes in the manner it had proposed by its signal which had been accepted and replied to by the slower craft.

Should the slower vessel ahead deem it unwise or unsafe for the other boat to pass it as has been proposed, she must immediately reply to the other's signal by sounding the danger signal. The overtaking boat must immediately cease all actions relating to passing, must reduce its speed so as not to get any closer to the vessel it had been overtaking, and wait for the safe reply to be given to its signal. There are times when the privileged boat will sound the danger signal, wait a moment or two, and then give the alternative passing signal to the boat to its rear. This will inform the overtaking boat that it was unsafe to pass on the side it had indicated it would but that it was alright to pass on the other side. While this is not normally done and is not specifically provided for in the rules, it is not uncommon and is quite logical. After all, the overtaken vessel has a better viewpoint as to what's going on in front than the overtaking boat. Should this happen, the overtaking boat must reply to the privileged boat's signal, using the same signal, and then proceed to accomplish the passing.

As in all other signalling situations, cross signals must never be used. All replies should be made with the same number and character of blasts as used by the initiating vessel, unless the danger signal is used instead. Anything else would prove confusing and contributing to a collision. Although privileged, the overtaken boat is prohibited from crossing the bow or in any way crowding in upon the course of a passing boat once signals have been exchanged.

ROUNDING BENDS

The foregoing paragraphs deal with the rules as they apply to boats in passing situations. The Rules of the Road also provide a special signal to be used when a motorboat approaches a blind bend in a channel. This situation exists when the approaching boat cannot see a boat on the other side of the bend because of the height of the banks or for any other existing reason. In such an instance, the boat must give a signal when it is within one-half mile of the bend. The prescribed signal consists of one long blast (from eight to ten seconds in duration) of its whistle. Should this signal be replied to by a similar blast from an unseen boat, normal whistle signals are then exchanged as soon as both boats are within sight of each other. If there is no reply, the signalling boat may assume that there is no unseen boat on the other side of the bend and that the channel is clear. It can then govern itself

accordingly and proceed on course. Of course, the prudent skipper will exercise greater than normal care and will proceed at only moderate speed until the bend has been cleared.

WHEN LEAVING A BERTH

A motorboat being moved from a berth does not have the right-of-way over any other boat which is passing in the channel or is in the open waters nearby. As she is about to move away from her berth, she is required to signal her intention by sounding a long blast on her whistle or horn. She may then proceed slowly and cautiously to move out toward open water. But she must be prepared to wait her turn as she has no privileged status in a crossing situation until she is already out in

open water and is fully in sight.

WHEN IN REVERSE

The Inland Rules provide a signal which is to be sounded when a boat's engine is in reverse and the boat is making sternway. When there are other boats in the vicinity, a boat making sternway is required to give a signal consisting of three short blasts on her whistle. There is no need to reply to such a signal on the part of another boat. However, if there is imminent danger involved, the danger signal should be sounded by an observing skipper.

WHEN UNDERWAY
IN POOR VISIBILITY

There are certain sound signals which must be given when visibility conditions are less than what may be considered normal. These special-situation signals are often referred to as "fog signals." However, they are just as applicable during periods of heavy mist, falling snow, heavy rains, or any other conditions which reduce visibility to no more than one mile. All power-driven water craft underway under such conditions of reduced visibility must sound one prolonged blast of her whistle (of 4- to 6-seconds duration) at intervals which are no more than one minute apart. If a power-driven boat is towing another boat under these conditions of low visibility, especially in fog, it must sound a signal consisting of one prolonged blast followed immediately by two one-second blasts, repeated at intervals of no more than one minute.

WHEN AT ANCHOR
IN POOR VISIBILITY

A boat which is at anchor during periods of fog or other visibility-reducing condition, either during the day or night, is required to ring a fog bell rapidly for about five seconds, again at intervals of no more than one minute.

The very same signal is required to be given by boats which are tied to a mooring buoy offshore from a marina. However, boats which are tied to a pier or wharf need not sound such signals unless they are hazardous to other boats by projecting out into an open channel.

SPEED IN BAD WEATHER

What is the speed limit permitted by law when a boat is cruising in weather which restricts visibility as described above? Well, the law is not quite decisive, setting the limit at a flexible "moderate speed." The rules go on to state, in a not very helpful way, that the speed at which a boat is run during bad weather should be such that the skipper demonstrates a careful regard to the existing circumstances and conditions. As a matter of practical safety, your boat should be operated at a speed which will give you the ability to stop within less than half the distance of visibility. This is a safe margin in which to avoid the risk of collision with another vessel or object.

Should a fog signal be heard coming from somewhere forward of the beam of your boat, legislation requires that your boat be stopped (providing it is safe to do so) and then proceed with extreme caution until there is absolutely no risk of collision.

GENERAL RULE

There is never any excuse for a motorboat not being properly equipped as regards lights, signals, etc. as called for by regulations. Also, there is never any excuse for a boat disobeying the Rules of the Road and other regulations ... *under normal operating conditions.* That is the one qualification to the rules of navigation. They may be, and they should be, disregarded if this disregard is essential to avoid immediate danger. The really important words in the preceding sentence are the last two ... *immediate danger.* The rules must not be disregarded just because perceptible danger exists, only when there is clearly immediate danger in strict adherence to the rules. Courts have ruled that in circumstances of immediate danger, strict adherence to a rule may be culpable fault. Boatmen are given quite a bit of latitude by this rule. However, be especially careful that it is not abused. The fact that adhering to the letter of the law may be inconvenient or the fact that there is a possibility of danger involved do not excuse a boatman from following the strict dictates of the regulation. A very real and immediate danger must exist ... and this is a rare situation.

U. S. COAST GUARD AUXILIARY

To promote greater safety afloat, the United-States Coast Guard Auxiliary offers three basic courses concerned with proper boat handling and good seamanship. All these courses are available to the public at no charge and are so designed that they relate specifically to the beginner.

The course in the handling of outboards consists of one lesson on the fundamental rules of boat handling, equipment requirements, and the common rules of courtesy when afloat.

A good follow-up to that initial one-lesson course is a slightly more extensive course, consisting of three lessons, which concerns itself with safe boating. This course includes aids to navigation and safety rules for both inboard and outboard operators.

Then there is an eight-lesson course on basic seamanship which is the most complete course given by the Auxiliary. This course covers items such as marlinspike seamanship, safety, and navigation. Those who successfully complete this course are awarded the United States Coast Guard Auxiliary Basic Seamanship Certificate.

U. S. POWER SQUADRONS

The United States Power Squadrons are an organization composed of experienced boatmen. They offer an extensive course of twelve lectures covering all phases of boat operation. For information regarding the locations of local classes and the times at which they are given, contact USPS Headquarters, P. O. Box 510, Englewood, New Jersey 07631. ●

CHAPTER TEN

Visual and Sound Signalling

■ Practically since its invention many years ago, radio has been the basic means of communication between ships at sea and between ships and shore. However, there are times when radiotelegraph and radiotelephone are not practical or desirable. Such times might be when military secrecy requires radio silence, when ships of different nationalities desire to communicate but find the differences in language too much of a barrier, etc. At such times, radio is supplemented by other means of transmitting and receiving messages. Of course, one of the instances where supplementary communication devices are a real necessity is when radio equipment breaks down. The supplementary forms of signalling are the visual means such as flag-hoist, flashing light, and semaphore.

It is true that the average skipper of a pleasure boat will rarely, if ever, need to make use of visual signals and most pleasure boats don't carry a set of signal flags aboard. However, a fundamental knowledge of visual signals could be of value. For one thing, this knowledge provides an extra margin of safety should an emergency arise and the boat's radio equipment should go out of commission at the very moment it is needed. Unlikely, yes; but pos-

sible. Also, think how your ego could be expanded by being able to read the signals being flown by any merchant ships or naval vessels in the area. You could explain to your "crew" and passenger-guests the meaning of the different flags being flown by foreign vessels coming in or going out; you could read and translate messages being flashed from one naval ship to another. What added pleasure and satisfaction would be yours ... you'd have a greater sense of really "belonging" to the world of boats and ships.

FLAG-HOIST

There is a set of international code flags which is prescribed for use in flag-hoist signalling. The set consists of a total of forty flags: twenty-six alphabetical flags, ten numeral pennants, three substitutes (sometimes called repeaters), and one answering pennant. Not only are the flags standardized in order to eliminate any possibility of confusion, but their colors are similarly prescribed. The only colors used for signal flags are red, white, blue, yellow, and black. The majority of flags consist of two of these colors. Only two of the alphabet flags are of one color: the letter "B" is a solid red and the letter "Q" is a solid yellow; four are made up of three colors: the letters "C", "T", "W" and the numeral "3"; two use four colors: the letter "Z" and the numeral "9". All the color combinations are selected and arranged to achieve maximum contrast, thereby lessening the chances for misinterpretation.

PROCEDURES OF FLAG-HOIST SIGNALLING

Flags and pennants of the International Code are flown either singly or in combinations of two or more. To transmit messages coherently, flags and pennants may be mixed as needed. For the sake of simplicity, it is best to fly one signal from one hoist at a time. The word *hoist* refers to one or more groups of flags that are being flown from one halyard. Flag signals are read in the same manner as the Chinese language, from the top down. Should two or more halyards be used from the same yardarm, the hoists are read from outboard inward as well as from the top down. When more than one group of flags and/or pennants is flown from the same hoist, each group must be separated from the others. As each group represents a separate signal, bunching all groups together without separation could prove very confusing.

Once a signal has been hoisted, it must be kept flying until the receiving vessel has acknowledged. It is quite obvious that visual signals must be clearly visible to the receiving vessel or shore station to whom it is being sent; otherwise the signals will serve no purpose whatsoever. So, when sending flag-hoist signals, be sure that each flag and pennant is displayed in such a manner that it stands out clearly, not being even partially hidden from view by halyard, sails, etc.

The following are some two-letter groups taken from the International Code of Signals:

FLAGS	MESSAGE
AE	....I must abandon my vessel
CJ	.....Do you require assistance?
CN	....I am unable to give assistance
JI	.....Are you aground?
JL	.....You are running the risk of going aground
JW	....I have sprung a leak
KN	....I cannot take you in tow
LN	....Light (name follows) has been extinguished
LR	....Bar is not dangerous
LS	....Bar is dangerous
NF	....You are running into danger
NG	....You are in a dangerous position
PD	....Your navigation light not visible
PT	....What is the state of the tide?
QX	....Request permission to anchor
UF	....Follow pilot boat (or vessel indicated)
UO	....You must not enter harbor
UT	....Where are you bound for?
YK	....I am unable to answer you signal
ZQ	....Your signal appears in-

correctly coded. Check and repeat the whole.

SIGNALLING WITH FLASHING LIGHT

This form of sending messages from ship to ship or from ship to shore is in wide use by naval forces. For one thing, it can convey messages much quicker than the flag-hoist method and, even more importantly, it permits the maintenance of radio silence when military secrecy requires such silence. This method of sending signals can also be very useful to the small-craft pleasure boatman. There is no need for the carrying of elaborate equipment ... an ordinary flashlight suffices. The only specialized equipment the skipper of a pleasure boat needs in order to send messages by means of a flashing light is the knowledge of the International Morse Code.

The International Morse Code, made up of *dots* and *dashes,* is used for sending messages via flashing light, the code being made up of short and long flashes of light. It takes time to learn and memorize the characters in the Morse Code; but anyone can do it and it may well prove worth while to expend the effort and time necessary. Once it is learned, and practiced from time to time, it will not be forgotten and may very well come in handy some day.

PROCEDURES OF FLASHING-LIGHT SIGNALLING

Naval vessels and merchant marine ships have professional signalmen aboard who are fully-trained in the formal procedures of establishing and conveying of communications by flashing light. A knowledge of the basic fundamentals which would aid in the event of an emergency is all the average boat owner need have.

When a boatman wants to establish flashing-light communication with another boat, he starts by training his light directly on the other and flashes the other boat's call letters (if they are known) or the signal "AA, AA, AA" etc. until the other boat answers. The other boat, upon observing the calling signal, answers by flashing the Morse Code signal for "TTTTT", etc. This answering signal is discontinued as soon as the calling signal is discontinued. Now, the boats are ready to receive and respond to flashing-light messages.

The Morse Code is used for relaying messages, as noted before. But there are certain letters and combinations thereof which have been established to give special procedural meanings. That is, they contain short messages within themselves. The following are some of the more basic signals and their meanings:

R (·—·) means "Message Received"

EEEEEE (·······) means that an error has been made; erase

RQ (·—·—·—) is the interrogative signal

C (—·—·) is the affirmative signal

As stated before, the average boatman won't have any regular purpose in using flashing-light as a means of communication. How-

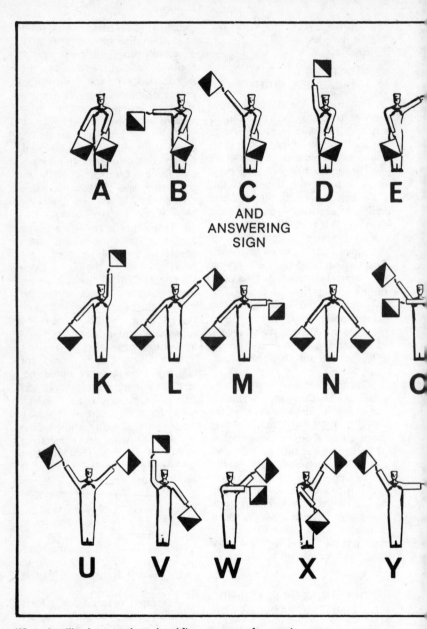

When signalling by semaphore, hand flags are most often used.

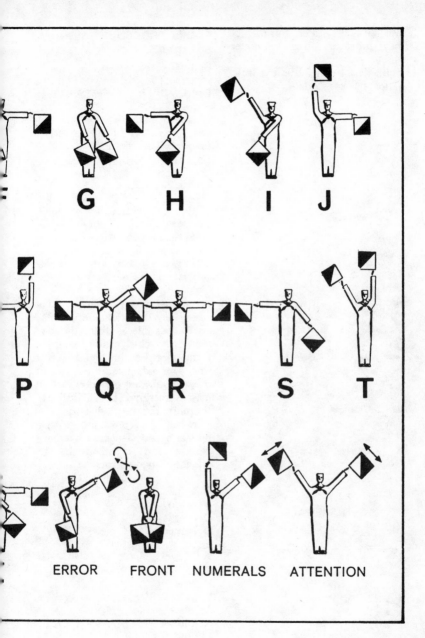

G H I J

P Q R S T

ERROR FRONT NUMERALS ATTENTION

ever, an ability to use this method may prove invaluable in emergency situations, especially at night. The following is the International Morse Code:

ALPHABET

A ·—
B —···
C —·—·
D —··
E ·
F ··—·
G ——·
H ····
I ··
J ·———
K —·—
L ·—··
M ——
N —·
O ———
P ·——·
Q ——·—
R ·—·
S ···
T —
U ··—
V ···—
W ·——
X —··—
Y —·——
Z ——··

NUMERALS

1 ·————
2 ··———
3 ···——
4 ····—
5 ·····
6 —····
7 ——···
8 ———··
9 ————·
0 —————

SIMPLE PROCEDURE SIGNALS

Period ·—·—·—
Comma ——··——
Interrogative ·—·——·— (RQ)
Distress Call ···———··· (SOS)
From —··· (DE)
Go ahead, transmit —·— (K)
Wait ·—··· (A & S run together)
Error ····· (series of E's)
Received ·—· (R)

SPACES

Between parts of the same letter . . . equal to one dot in time

Between two letters . . . equal to three dots in time

Between two words . . . equal to five dots in time

Because of an accent or other emergency stress situation, it may not be possible to distinctly communicate valuable life-saving information. Recognizing the fact that even when radio equipment may be working perfectly well, it may sometimes be difficult to transmit coherent messages because of the above problems, a phonetic code language has been devised and is standard. The phonetic language code is:

A alpha
B bravo
C charlie
D delta
E echo
F foxtrot
G golf
H hotel
I india
J juliet
K kilo
L lima
M mike

N november
O oscar
P papa
Q quebec
R romeo
S sierra
T tango
U uniform
V victor
W whisky
X x-ray
Y yankee
Z zulu

SIGNALLING
WITH
SEMAPHORE

To transmit messages via semaphore, a pair of hand flags is normally used. These help because of their great visibility. However, only the hands could be used or simple handkerchiefs if the signals are being sent over somewhat short distances.

The alphabet used for semaphore signalling is the ordinary English range of 26 letters and all numerals are spelled out. The letters are indicated by the position of the two hands of the sender, each hand being held in any one of eight positions, as shown in the illustration. A very important position for the hands is the one in which both hands are held all the way down in front. This is the *break sign* and is used to separate words and double letters in the same word.

PROCEDURES
OF SEMAPHORE
SIGNALLING

The sender will initiate the sending of semaphore signals by first indicating his intention by sending the signal K 1, using any means of communication available. The receiving ship, if able to communicate by semaphore, will respond with the letter C. If the intended receiving ship is unable to communicate by semaphore, the reply signal is YS 1. The sender uses his flags (or hands) to send each letter distinctly, moving smoothly without pause from the positions of one letter directly to the next until he comes to the end of a word. Then he drops his hands to the break position and waits for the receiver to indicate that the word has been received and understood. This is done by the sender transmitting the signal letter C. The message can then be continued. At the end of the completed message, the signal AR is sent.

Aboard recreational boats, semaphore signalling has distinct advantages. Most pleasure boats do not carry a set of flag-hoist signals as part of their normal equipment. Semaphore permits a boatman to communicate with other ships at greater distances than he could with only his voice, even through a megaphone or other amplifying device. There is no special equipment necessary and is certainly a better way of sending signals than a flashing light during the daylight hours. Its one great disadvantage is that it requires the learning of the code and a great deal of practice in order to attain a degree of proficiency. Of course, like flag-hoists, it is totally useless at night. ●

CHAPTER ELEVEN

Piloting and Navigating

■ Simple navigation is accomplished through the use of a nautical chart, a nautical compass, and a parallel rule. This is the only equipment needed, besides the knowledge of how to use them. Exact charts of the coastal and inland waterways of the United States are painstakingly prepared by the U. S. Corps of Engineers and/or the U. S. Coast and Geodetic Survey Office. These charts can be obtained from either of these two sources. The navigational charts clearly supply all the information needed with which to successfully and, more importantly, safely navigate in the waters of the United States. Figures indicating the average low water measurement for the area covered by specific charts are listed. Other details of vital information listed in the charts include the locations and types of buoys, danger areas which may contain rocks or other obstructions, areas of dangerously shallow water, and prominent landmarks, such as church steeples and factory smokestacks, which can be of tremendous help in locating one's position. The vertical lines on the chart show longitude (true north-south) while the chart's horizontal lines show latitude (true east-west).

Because of all the infinite amount of information contained on these charts, it is necessary that many abbreviations and symbols be used. There just wouldn't be enough room on any manageable chart to spell out everything that has to be shown. For example, the location of a black buoy is indicated by the use of a black diamond-shaped symbol; the location of a red buoy is indicated by the use of a magenta-colored diamond-shaped symbol. All buoys, whatever their color, are shown as diamond-shaped symbols. A day beacon is indicated on the charts as a triangle-shaped symbol, with the abbreviation "BN" appearing alongside.

In order for a compass to be considered adequate for navigational purposes, it should be graduated in units of five to ten degrees. One thing that must constantly be kept in mind is that the compass arrow always points toward the magnetic north pole, not toward the geographical north pole. The magnetic north pole is not exactly the same as the geographical north pole. Not only that, but the degree difference between the magnetic north pole and the geographical north pole varies depending on the location of the compass. The somewhat simple explanation for this is that the earth is a sphere, not a square or rectangular flat object. If the earth were indeed flat, the angle between the two would never change. The location of the geographic north pole is a constant. Actually, the location of the magnetic north pole is likewise a constant. However, the relation of an observer on a spherical surface to it varies. The difference in degrees between the direction in which the compass points and the geographic north pole is called the compass variation.

PLOTTING COURSES

Charts are designed and laid out on the basis of using the geographic north pole. Only by knowing the amount of variation, at a particular location, between the magnetic north pole as indicated by the arrow point on the compass and the geographic north pole shown on the chart, is a boatman capable of plotting his course. The compass rosette on a chart is the indicator of this variation. The outer circle of the rosette points in the direction of true north (the geographic north pole). The inner circle of the rosette indicates the direction of the magnetic north pole. Let us assume that a course of due east is what the skipper desires. Geographically, according to the chart, the direction is 90 degrees. However, if the variation indicated by the outer and inner circles of the compass rosette is 10 degrees, then the skipper knows that, in order to head due east from his location, he must take a compass heading of 100 degrees.

A somewhat more complicated case occurs if the plotting is done between two points on the chart and then the direction is determined. Using a parallel rule, a line is first drawn between the two points in question. The rule is then extended until it passes through the center of the nearest compass rose. The place at which the rule bisects the inner circle is the compass heading needed to pilot between the two points.

Far too often for comfort, you may find that it is not possible, because of submerged obstacles or other reasons, to travel in a straight line in order to get from one point of location on the chart to another. This requires that several compass headings be taken. The method to be employed in these instances is hopping from buoy to buoy as you make progress in the general direction of your target area. Upon reaching the first buoy along the prescribed path, the direction is altered until the next buoy is sighted, and so on. In the event that there are not a sufficient number of buoy markers along the route that is desired, or if the location of the buoy markers is such that following them would lead to a wasteful, roundabout course, then it is important that the skipper know the speed of his boat and make use of that knowledge. For the sake of citing an example, let us assume that the first leg of the journey is to be taken at a compass heading of 87 degrees for three miles and the second section of the journey at a heading of 115 degrees for six miles. If the boat is travelling at a speed of 30 miles per hour, it will cover the first 3-mile leg of the journey in six minutes. Then, maintaining the same rate of

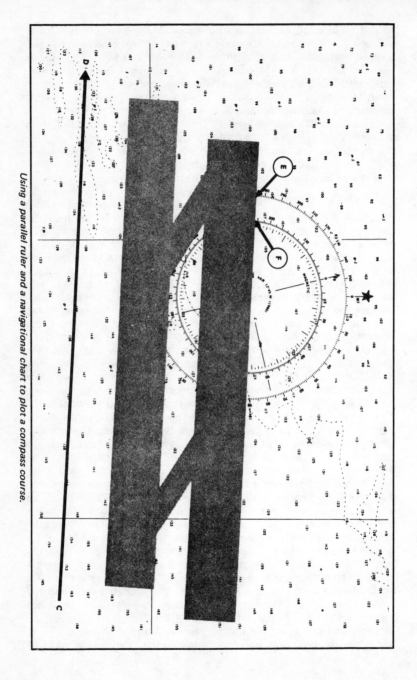

Using a parallel ruler and a navigational chart to plot a compass course.

speed, the skipper can turn to a heading of 115 degrees and arrive at his destination in twelve minutes.

Compasses, their points being magnetic, are greatly influenced by the presence of steel and/or iron in their proximity. Errors in compass reading caused by the presence of such metallic objects is known as compass deviation. The reader of a compass must always be alert to spot the presence of steel and/or iron that would cause any such deviation. Otherwise, his readings will be wrong and he will send the boat off on an incorrect heading and, conceivably, get himself and everybody else aboard the boat . . . lost. Most compasses are equipped so that they are adjustable to remove any such deviation.

MEASURING TIME, SPEED, AND DISTANCE

The distances between any two points on a chart are measured in terms of nautical miles, rather than land (statute) miles. A nautical mile is 1.15 longer than a statute mile. Should the speedometer on your boat be calibrated in statute miles-per-hour, take the time and spend a little effort in the making of a conversion table, showing statute miles-per-hour and their equivalent in nautical miles-per-hour. Once out to sea, doing this in advance can save you a great deal of confusion and lost time.

In order to pre-determine the expected time-elapse of a projected cruise, total up the distances that have been plotted on the chart. Every chart has, beside all the other symbols and bits of information needed to plot a safe course, a scale showing the relationship between inches on the chart and the miles into which they are translated. When the total distance is determined, divide the distance by the average speed at which you expect your boat to travel. The resulting answer will be the time it will take you to make your cruise. For example, a 30-mile voyage made at an average speed of 20 miles-per-hour will consume a total of one and one-half hours (speed multiplied by time equals distance).

The accuracy of a speedometer should be checked from time to time. This can easily be done by running the boat over a course the length of which is known. There are many shorelines which have stakes which indicate an officially measured mile. Pick out the stakes you will use in your timing test. As you approach the first marker, run your boat up to its usual cruising speed. Using a stopwatch, record the time that elapses from the time you hit the first marker until you've passed the second marker. Because a boat's performance can easily be affected by the vagaries of water current and the forces of winds, it is best to run this measured-mile course a minimum of three times. After the third run, average the time needed to run the mile in terms of seconds and divide this average number of seconds into 3,600 (the number of seconds in one hour). The resulting answer will be the actual speed in miles-per-hour of the boat over the measured mile. The difference between the speedometer reading (which had been carefully recorded by a member of your "crew" during the runs) and the actual speed (as determined by the stop-watch test), if any, is the amount of speedometer error that can be expected at cruising speed.

TIDES AND CURRENTS

The action of incoming and outgoing tides is caused by the gravitational pull of the moon and, to a somewhat lesser extent, the sun. During the course of each twenty-four hour period of each day, there are two flood tides and two ebb tides (flood tides being the incoming tides and ebb tides being the outgoing tides). Because of the rotation of the earth around the sun during each twenty-four hour period and the rotation of the earth on its axis which alters the relative position of any one specific location on earth to the sun, the moon rises fifty minutes later every day in any one location on earth. Therefore, the timing of the tides in that location changes by that same fifty minutes each and every day.

The positions of the sun and the moon in relation to each other also exert an influence on tides. Spring tides occur when the moon and the sun are in a direct line to each other. This happens at the incidence of a new moon and also when there is a full moon visible. This sun-moon relationship results in very high tides, bordering on flooding. The very opposite occurs when the moon and the sun

are both at right angles to the earth (during periods of the first and last quarters of the moon). At these times, there are exceptionally low tides, called neap tides.

The flow of the tides results in currents being present in the water. Tides are actually the vertical (up and down) motion of the water; currents are the movement of water in a horizontal manner. When leaving a dock at a time when there is present a two mile-per-hour current which has been caused by an ebb tide, a boat will travel at a speed which is two miles-per-hour faster in relation to the bottom. Obviously, the reverse is similarly true. A boat heading into a two mile-per-hour current will move at a speed two miles-per-hour slower in relation to the bottom. Currents are far more difficult to measure than are tides. Currents are easily influenced by wind and flooding. A boatman should never assume that tables which list the prevailing currents for a particular area are absolutely accurate.

In the piloting of a boat, consideration must be given to the effect of the prevailing current. For example, a two hour north-south cruise in a two miles-per-hour east-west current will result in a landing four miles west of the expected destination, unless steps are taken to counter the effect of the current. In this instance, the boat must be steered in an easterly arc, eliminating the effect of the current pushing the boat off course toward the west.

AIDS TO NAVIGATION

Any and all obstructions in the

water are, of course, dangerous to boats in their area. But by far the most dangerous are the great number of shoals and rocks that are hidden from view beneath the surface of the water. Those obstructions which can be seen above the surface of the water may be a hindrance to the boatman but they are nowhere near as great a threat to his safety and the safety of his boat and passengers.

Navigators sometimes use natural landmarks such as church steeples and industrial smokestacks as reference points in helping them locate themselves regarding their position. However, these natural landmarks may be too widely spaced apart to be relied on too heavily. In order to protect defenseless boatmen from the unseen perils lurking beneath the surface of the water, and to make it possible for them to direct their courses with accuracy and safety, governmental agencies and private citizens have established, and maintain, *aids to navigation.*

An *aid to navigation* is just about any object which is created and made by man (any gender of humankind) and is placed in such a spot on or near the water that it will help the boatman define the location of his vessel or indicate to him the safe and proper course he is to follow. Included as items known as aids to navigation are buoys, day beacons, lights, lighthouses, lightships, radiobeacons, fog signals and a number of electronic signals. These items should always be referred to as *aids to navigation* rather than *navigational aids*. The latter term, while also covering these items, is used in a much broader sense to cover charts, instruments, devices, methods, etc. In the following pages, we will be discussing aids to navigation.

ESTABLISHMENT AND MAINTENANCE

In order for an aid to navigation to be established in any body of water falling under the jurisdiction of the Federal government of the United States, there must first be established economic justification for the aid. That means that there must be a "reasonable" amount of traffic on the specific body of water to warrant the establishment of an aid to navigation, and its continuing maintenance. These aids, under the law, cannot be established and maintained for the benefit of only an occasional boat that may pass that way or for the convenience of a few boats belonging to local boatmen.

Once it has been determined that there is, indeed, economic justification for the establishment and maintenance of an aid to navigation in a particular body of water, the actual aid is so designed that it can be seen and/or heard over the greatest practicable area. Any differences in their structural design are present only because the aid's purpose is to meet the requirements and physical conditions of the site on which the aid is placed. In other words, it all depends on the specific needs of a location whether a buoy will be established or a beacon; whether there will be a minor light or a major lighthouse.

Once established, it is the responsibility of the United States Coast Guard to properly maintain aids to navigation. That is, those aids to navigation which have been established on those waters of the United States which are under the jurisdiction of the Federal government. That includes all coastal waters as well as rivers, bays, sounds, lakes, etc. which are navigable from the sea as well as those same types of bodies of water which, while not navigable from the sea, do not lie completely within the boundaries of any one state. The Coast Guard may also maintain aids to navigation wherever they are needed by any branch of our armed forces.

As stated earlier, private citizens may also establish aids to navigation. These aids, and those which may be established by other than Federal governmental agencies (state, municipal, etc.) as well as Federal agencies other than the Coast Guard (Army, Navy, etc.), are all termed and listed as *private* aids. Before being established in any waters under Federal jurisdiction, these private aids must be approved by the United States Coast Guard. They must follow the same pattern as Federal aids and, in the event it is intended that a fixed structure be built, a permit must first be issued by the Army Corps of Engineers.

Where the Federal government does not have jurisdiction, such as on waters which fall entirely within the boundaries of a single state and are not navigable from the sea, the state is responsible for establishing and maintaining the needed aids to navigation. To avoid confusion and thereby create a situation that would promote exactly that which is contrary to the purpose of the aids, there is a uniform system of aids to navigation. So, it doesn't matter what waters you may be boating on ... channels will all be marked the same way, etc.

LEGAL PROTECTION OF AIDS

The law clearly and definitely protects all aids to navigation, no matter by whom established and maintained. Not only is it against the laws of common sense to damage or in any way cause hindrance to the proper operation of an aid, it is also a criminal offense punishable under the laws of the United States. It is against Federal law to deface, alter, move, or destroy any aid to navigation, no matter where it may be located or who may have put it there. All boatmen must be certain never, never to tie a boat to marker buoys, daybeacons, or any light structure. Neither should a boatman anchor his boat in such a way as to block an aid from the view of passing vessels.

In the event your boat accidentally collides with and damages an aid to navigation, common sense, common courtesy, and the law require that you report the incident to the proper authority with no undue delay. Also, should you detect any missing or malfunctioning aid, you should report it just as quickly as possible. This cooperation will inure to your own safety as well as the safety of others. The report should be made as soon as you reach port unless the missing or malfunctioning aid represents a serious, present threat to navigation. In that case, the report should be immediately made via radio or other signalling device.

TYPES OF AIDS

Buoys: These are objects which float in the water, being moored or anchored to the bottom. They have distinctive and varied shapes and colors, depending on their location and their purpose in being there. Some buoys are equipped with visual, audible, and/or electronic signal devices, depending on any special purpose.

Daybeacons: These are fixed-position, unlighted structures which may be made up of a single pile or as a series of multiple piles. Daybeacons are usually equipped with daymarkers, such as pointers or signboards. These daymarkers may be designed with distinctive colors and/or shapes, depending on the information they are meant to give.

Lightships: These are vessels which are moored or anchored at certain specific locations and are specially equipped to serve as aids to navigation. The equipment consists of lights, sound signals, and radiobeacons among other supplementary aids.

There are many other types of aids to navigation such as Lights, Fog Signals, Ranges, Radiobeacons, and Electronic Navigation Systems. However, they are too numerous and require more description and explanation than we have room for in this book. As with the subject of boat handling

covered in HOW TO HANDLE A BOAT, the reader is urged to read Chapman's, *Piloting, Seamanship and Small Boat Handling* which covers this fascinating and extremely important topic in great detail.

BUOYS

As indicated above, these are objects which float in the water, being moored or anchored to the bottom. They are placed at specific locations to act as aids to navigation and have shapes and colors that are geared to their location and purpose. On navigational charts, they are indicated by special symbols and letters. These tell the chart reader the shape of the buoy, its color, and any visual and/or sound signals with which it may be equipped. Buoys come in a variety of sizes, ranging from the small, sixth-class buoy which projects only a few feet from the water all the way up to the new super-sized buoys which measure about forty feet in diameter with superstructures which rise above the surface of the water to a height of thirty or more feet. There are buoys which are lighted, unlighted, equipped with sound, and combination buoys which give off both audible and visual signals. At the present time, the Coast Guard has the responsibility of maintaining approximately 21,000 unlighted buoys and 3,700 lighted and combination buoys in waters which are under Federal jurisdiction. Of course, there are uncounted other buoys which are maintained by individual states and private agencies in waters which do not fall into the classification of *navigable waters.*

UNLIGHTED BUOY SHAPES

Unlighted buoys are classified by their shape and are given specific names. *Can buoys* have an above-water appearance that is cylindrical in shape, much like a can or barrel which is floating vertically, with its flat end upward. *Nun buoys* look like a cylinder which is topped with pointed-end cone, the pointed end being up. This point may either be sharp or rounded ... it doesn't matter. Both of these unlighted buoys come in standardized sizes but it is unimportant whether the boatman knows these sizes or not. The only things the boatman or pilot must know is the reason for the different shapes and their meanings in relation to navigation. This subject will be discussed in somewhat greater detail a bit later in this chapter.

LIGHTED BUOYS

Lighted buoys, as well as sound buoys, are not classified as to their shapes but rather, they are described by their visual and audible signals. The lights on these buoys come in a variety of colors and have varied flashing characteristics, known as phase characteristics. The color of the light and its phase characteristic imparts specific information to a boat's pilot. Most lighted buoys are now equipped with automatic controls which turn the light on and off with the respective approach of sunset and sunrise. The only colors used for the lights on these buoys are red, green, and white. Other colors won't show.

SOUND BUOYS

These buoys transmit a characteristic sound signal which aids in their being located by a boat's pilot when, because of darkness or weather, their visibility has been reduced. There are a number of different sounds used. The purpose for the difference in sound signals is to differentiate between the different aids to navigation that may be located near to each other.

Bell buoys are made up of steel floats on which stand short skeleton towers. The bell is mounted in the tower and is operated, in most cases, by the motion of the water in which it is located. As the waves or ground swells cause the buoy to roll, loosely hung tappers are set to clanging. These tappers are so arranged that the sound signal given will be a single note, sounded at irregular intervals. In sheltered waters where there is not much wave or groundswell action, bells are operated by electric batteries. In these instances, the signal is sounded at regular intervals. As you can readily see, the more moderate operating costs of the non-battery operated bell, as well as its equal effectiveness, makes it the more numerously used. *Gong buoys* are similar in construction to the bell buoy except that the signal is transmitted by a set of gongs rather than a bell. Then there is the *whistle buoy* which gives still another distinctive sound signal which is very useful at night and during periods of fog. The rolling motion of the buoy in the water

FEDERAL
WATERWAY MARKERS

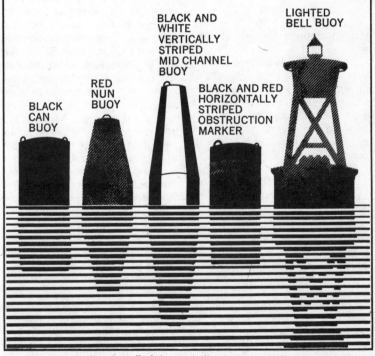

BLACK AND
WHITE
VERTICALLY
STRIPED
MID CHANNEL
BUOY

LIGHTED
BELL BUOY

RED
NUN
BUOY

BLACK AND RED
HORIZONTALLY
STRIPED
OBSTRUCTION
MARKER

BLACK
CAN
BUOY

Buoys are the "signposts" of the sea, indicating courses, danger zones, etc.

produces compressed air which, in turn, produces the whistling sound that is heard. This type of buoy is practical only in the open seas where normal waves and groundswells can cause the buoy to roll; it is not practical in sheltered waters.

DAYBEACONS

These are fixed-position, unlighted aids to navigation which may be located either on shore or in relatively shallow waters. The design and construction of daybeacons varies greatly, depending on their location and also on how far a distance they are intended to be seen. In order to serve their purpose as effective aids to navigation, daybeacons need to be properly identified. This is accomplished through the use of daymarks or pointers.

A basic, simple daybeacon consists of a single pile which is driven into the bottom and protrudes above the surface of the water. It has a daymark at or near its top to identify its purpose. The pile may be composed of wood, concrete, or metal. There is also a more elaborate daybeacon known as the "dolphin". This consists of three piles (or five piles, with one central pile and four others surrounding it) which are spread apart at the bottom but come together at the top, with wire cables holding the tops together.

LIGHTSHIPS

These are ships which are anchored or moored at specific, charted locations. They have distinctive markings as well as being designed distinctively. These aids to navigation are equipped with fog signals, radiobeacons, and, naturally, with lights. Their dominant purpose is to mark the entrances to important harbors, to warn of dangerous shoals which exist in much-travelled waters, and to serve as departure marks for both ocean-going and coastal traffic.

Essentially, they serve the same purpose as lighthouses. However, lightships can be located in areas where it is totally impractical, if not indeed impossible, to build lighthouses.

THE LATERAL BUOYAGE SYSTEM

This is a uniformly-used system employing a simple arrangement of differently shaped, colored, numbered, and lighted buoys to show the proper way of entering and leaving a harbor. To preclude the possibility of there being any confusion or misunderstanding regarding what is meant by "entering and leaving a harbor", the following system has been established: all boats will be considered as coming in from seaward if they are proceeding in a southerly direction along the Atlantic coast, in a north-westerly direction along the Gulf coast, and in a northerly direction along the Pacific coast. In other words, any ship sailing around the coastline of the United States in a clockwise direction is considered to be coming in from seaward.

Buoys are to the sea what road signs are to highways on land . . . they are signposts. Depending on their color, number, shape, and characteristics, they indicate the presence of danger zones or merely show the best course to steer to get to a certain destination . . . the best course always being the safest course.

As was stated a bit earlier, buoys are aids to navigation which primarily show the proper way of entering or leaving a harbor. Red-colored buoys are always "nuns", being conical in shape and always bear an even number (2, 4, 6, etc.). Nun buoys should always be kept to the starboard side when entering a harbor. The nautical expression of "Red — Right — Returning" is used to remind the pilot that red buoys are passed on your right when coming in from seaward. Black buoys are always "cans" and are odd (1, 3, 5, etc.) numbered. Can buoys should be off the port side when proceeding into a harbor.

The combinatioof red buoys to the starboard and black buoys off the port clearly define a marine roadway, or channel. When leaving the docking area, heading seaward, the positions of the buoys are reversed. Red buoys should be off the port, and black buoys off the starboard. It would be wise to remember that the same channel is generally used by both incoming and outgoing vessels. Therefore, the prudent pilot, when coming into the docking area, will keep as far to the right as possible, near the red buoys.

There are many other types of buoys, each used for a specific purpose as a further aid to navigation. A buoy with red and black horizontal stripes indicates an obstruction or a junction. It can be passed on either side if used to show a danger zone. Just keep clear of the immediate area in which the buoy is located. An obstruction buoy used as a junction marker has a red or black top band symbolizing the direction of the best channel to be used. From seaward, the red top acts as a regular red buoy and should be kept to the starboard. By doing this, a channel on the buoy's left is indicated. The opposite is true if the buoy has a black top stripe. Channel buoys are black-and-white vertically striped buoys and may appear in any shape. They inform the pilot that he is steering too far toward the center of the channel.

Another aid to navigation are range lights. These work much the same as runway lights at an airport. They are generally visible from only one direction and, when aligned, they indicate a safe course to follow. Range lights may be either fixed or flashing and may be colored white, red, or green.

LIGHTHOUSES

An aid to navigation which is familiar to all lovers of paintings of marine landscapes is the lighthouse. These solidly-built, fixed-position structures serve to warn boat pilots of danger spots and also serve to guide pilots into harbor entrances. Each lighthouse is painted differently and has its own characteristic color of light or frequency of flash. Marine charts describe each lighthouse so that none can be mistaken for another. Most generally, lighthouses are equipped with fog signals and radiobeacons.

READING THE WATER

This is not in any sense an "aid to navigation"; accurate water reading is, rather, a navigational aid which is acquired only through experience. On the open sea, the water responds to the pushing force of the prevailing winds. For example, a light breeze ranging from four to seven miles-per-hour results in wavelets of about six inches, with unbroken crests. They are barely noticeable. However, a strong wind blowing at from twenty-five to thirty-one miles-per-hour will cause the formation of large 13-foot waves with crests of white foam.

As a boat approaches the shoreline during rough weather, the waves will begin to swell and break. Coming toward the docking area from the leeward side is considerably easier and safer. The land, to some extent, shelters the water from the full effect of the wind and, thereby, offers the boat some protection from the elements. It can be a dreadfully frightening experience to approach the shore with the wind at your back. Should you be caught in high waves, under no circumstances are you to attempt to outrace them to the shore. It is a race you are most likely to lose ... and in a most sorrowful fashion. Attempting to outrace a high wave can only result in the boat going up the seaward side of the wave, coming down over the crest, with the bow plunging straight under the water. Instead of racing the wave, try to have the boat's speed match the velocity of the wave. In this way, it is possible to ride the same wave position all the way in to shore.

River reading is different from ocean reading. There are many more indicators of the water's flow in a river. The direction in which the current is going can be seen by the movement of any debris that may be floating on the surface of the water. Also, fast-flowing deep water is darker in color than the water at the surface. Underwater obstacles can be more easily spotted in a river, as the water ripples around them. Swift downstream flowing water, narrowing over a rock bottom, forms a V-shaped channel. Always steer in the center of the channel; it contains the deeper water. An upstream V-shaped channel, on the other hand, should be avoided entirely. It indicates a large obstacle that is close to the surface.

When running past a tributary, attempt to keep heading with the main stream. Frequently, a tributary carries mud along with it and deposits the sediment when it comes in contact with a larger body of water. The quieter water off to the sides is shallower due to the deposits.

The best way to run a river is to always steer with the darker deep water. If the river bends, the deepest water will be at the outer edge of the curve. That's where you should be.

After a storm, always be on the lookout for debris that may have been washed from the shore into the river. Proceed at relatively slow speed. In this way, any floating debris that happens to be struck by your boat will merely glance off the hull. ●

CHAPTER TWELVE

Weather

■ Before starting out on a cruise which will last more than just a few hours and will take the boat and its human cargo out of local waters, the prudent boatman checks all possible sources of weather information so he will be familiar with weather conditions awaiting him at his destination or enroute. A weather map is one of the better sources of this kind of information. There are some boatmen who subscribe to and receive weekly compilations of daily weather maps. These are prepared by the National Weather Service and are mailed to subscribers. Most pleasure boat owners, however, get their weather map information from their daily, local newspapers. These are dependable as they, too, are drawn from the master weather charts of the National Weather Service. The weather map makes available to the reader of one, a view of weather conditions covering a rather large area of the earth's surface. There are many symbols, lines, and figures used to indicate weather conditions and these are sure to prove very puzzling to the beginner in weather-map reading. However, by doing a bit of research into what all the indicators mean and a little studying and analyzing of weather maps, the interested boatman will soon be able to frame a picture of what is in store for him on any given day in any given location as regards weather.

FORECASTING FROM NATURE

Weather, of course, completely surrounds us. But where did the weather that we are experiencing in our particular part of the country form? Generally speaking, weather forms in the west and moves in an easterly direction. Therefore, someone living in the Middle Atlantic states has some idea of what type of weather he may expect to have in the near future if he knows what type of weather is being experienced by people living in the northern Pacific states. Of course, the timing of the weather, in travelling from west to east, depends to a great extent on prevailing wind velocity, natural obstructions such as mountain ranges, etc.

A fundamental fact regarding the earth's movement on its axis as it revolves around the sun is that the sun always rises in the east and always sets in the west. As basic as it is, it is important to remember. By carefully regarding the sky at sunset, it is possible to get a preview of what the weather will be like the following day. For example, if the sky is a brilliant red at sunset time, it is a good bet

Initial indication of approaching warm front are high, tufted cirrus clouds.

The warm front second stage is heralded by cloud cover forming cirrostratus.

Heavy cumulus clouds are often harbingers of violent thunderstorms when the humid, overheated late afternoon air becomes unstable.

Cumulonimbus clouds with characteristic anvil top denote violent thunderstorm.

Banded Altocumulus; "mackerel sky" warns of approaching cold front and squalls.

The approach of clear, cold weather is signified by breaking up fractocumulus.

Stratocumulus will disperse soon after sunrise becoming fair weather cumulus.

that there will be fair weather the following day. Should there be approaching clouds which are interfering with the setting sun and creating a sunset which is bright yellow in color, the indication is that the next day very likely is going to be windy. If instead of a bright yellow sunset we get a pale yellow sunset, the possibility is good that there will be rain falling on your head the following day. A brewing storm is quite reliably forecast by a sunset which is hidden by white clouds.

The color of the sunrise is an equally indicative sign of oncoming weather. If the sky is red at sunrise, you will probably experience bad weather before the day is through; should the sun rise out of a horizon which is gray, fair weather is probably in the offing.

The man in the moon is also a weather forecaster. When there is a halo noted around the surface of the moon, this halo is caused by the light of the moon being diffused through a cover of clouds. When this occurs, rain and/or wind is a good possibility.

Clouds figure very prominently in the forecasting of coming weather. Their density, type, color, and formation are indicators of what type of weather we can expect and are used to a great extent by those who are charged with the responsibility of predicting weather conditions in specific locations at specific times, or approximations thereof.

There are ten principal types of clouds which are defined in the International Cloud Classification, even though there are an infinite number of shapes and forms which clouds take. The ten types that are defined are all derived from three basic cloud forms. These are: 1) Streak clouds which are made up of extraordinarily tiny particles of ice. These particles often appear as trails which has caused them to be called, at times, mares' tails; 2) Sheet clouds which are in the main produced by slow-moving, widely-distributed rise of uncommonly stable air; 3) Heap clouds which are just the opposite of sheet clouds. These are the result of unstable air which is loaded with narrow, fast-moving bubbles, causing strong updrafts.

The ten principal types of clouds are:

1—CIRRUS.

2—CIRROCUMULUS.

3—CIRROSTRATUS.

4—ALTOCUMULUS.

5—ALTOSTRATUS.

6—NIMBOSTRATUS.

7—STRATOCUMULUS.

8—STRATUS.

9—CUMULUS.

10—CUMULONIMBUS.

The definitions of these clouds can be found in the 1956 edition of the International Cloud Atlas. They are not given here because they are not of such great importance and space is limited. However, it would do no harm, and might do some good, if all boatmen learned to identify the different clouds and their formations.

For our purpose here, a generalization about clouds is sufficient. Delicate, fluffy clouds hold little water and, therefore, do not present a threat of bad weather. Rather, they indicate fair weather and moderate breezes. The darker the color of the clouds, the more brisk the coming wind. Small, black clouds are an omen that rain is on its way. Light clouds moving rapidly under darker, heavier clouds foretell of wind and rain. Thunderstorms are usually announced by gray clouds with bulbous tops. The rapid formation of dense, vertical clouds can also indicate a coming thunderstorm. One aspect of cloud formations which is important to note is whether the clouds are increasing or decreasing in number and also if they are rising or getting lower.

STORM SIGNALS

On January 1, 1958, the U. S. Weather Bureau put into effect a simple system of Coastal Warning Displays. This was accomplished after thorough consultation with many groups interested in the subject, such as yacht clubs, shipping agencies and others having coastal interests. The system incorporates the use of only four separate signals for daylight hours and four separate lantern signals for nightime hours, or whenever visibility is low. The four signals are used for the following categories of warnings: small craft, gale, storm, and hurricane.

It is just impossible to emphasize strongly enough that these coastal warnings are merely supplementary to the written and broadcasted warnings which are given immediate distribution by varied media. The visual coastal warning signals we are discussing here cannot possibly supply such vital information as the time, intensity, duration, and direction of oncoming storms. The following are the signals:

Small Craft Warning: A single, solitary red pennant by day and a single red light directly above a white light at night or other periods of darkness. These signals are displayed when winds of over thirty-eight miles-per-hour velocity are forecast. Winds of such strength make the operation of small craft in the area dangerous.

Gale Warning: This signal consists of two red pennants flown one above the other during the day; a white light over a red light during periods of darkness. This signal is shown when the forecast calls for winds ranging from 38 to 54 miles-per-hour.

Storm Warning: This signal is used to indicate the forecast of winds ranging from 55 to 73 miles-per-hour. It consists of a single square red flag with a black center by day and two red lights, one above the other, at night.

Hurricane Warning: This is probably the most-feared of all storms, especially at sea. That is why the signal for this warning is the most dreaded one that a boatman can see. It consists of two red flags, each with a black center, flying directly above one another during daylight hours; at night, the hurricane warning consists of a white light sandwiched between

SMALL CRAFT

Daytime: RED PENNANT
Nighttime: RED LIGHT OVER
  WHITE LIGHT

Winds as high as 33 knots and sea conditions considered dangerous to small crafts.

GALE

Daytime: TWO RED PENNANTS
Nighttime: WHITE LIGHT OVER
  RED LIGHT

Winds between 34 and 47 knots.

STORM

Daytime: SQUARE RED FLAG
  WITH BLACK SQUARE
  CENTERED
Nighttime: TWO RED LIGHTS

Winds 48 knots and above no matter how high the wind speed. If the winds are connected with a hurricane, storm warnings indicate winds be-between 48 and 63 knots.

HURRICANE

Daytime: TWO SQUARE RED
  FLAGS WITH BLACK SQUARES
  CENTERED
Nighttime: WHITE LIGHT
  BETWEEN TWO RED LIGHTS

Winds of 64 knots and higher, displayed only in connection with a hurricane.

two red lights. This signal indicates that winds in excess of 74 miles-per-hour are expected and is a signal for all vessels to get out of the water if at all possible. If not possible, batten down the hatches!

By Weather Bureau definition, *Small Craft Warnings* are intended for small boats, yachts, tugs, barges with little freeboard, or any other low-powered craft. The National Weather Bureau broadcasts storm warnings and advisories over specially designated U. S. Naval and Coast Guard radio stations. These are broadcast on a regular, almost continuous basis. There are some commercial radio stations which transmit marine forecasts but these are done at somewhat irregular intervals.

FOG

Fog, to a far greater extent than the darkness that comes with the night, is one of the major enemies of the boatman. The falling of darkness with the coming of night is a fully-expected, natural occurrence and the average boatman is prepared for the resultant loss of visibility. But fog, whether by day or night, reduces visibility while also making the lighting of lamps almost useless. Light will just not cut through thick fog as it will through clear darkness. Fog is usually the result of a hot humid air mass being cooled as it passes over land or water. During daylight hours, fog is very often burned away as the sun warms the water and land. Therefore, it would seem possible to avoid being enveloped by fog

by simply steering one's boat into warmer waters.

However, it is not always easy to find warmer waters nearby and, even if it were, the boat would still have to travel through the fog to get there. From all practical points of view, a boat caught in a fog stays caught in that fog for quite a spell. At times like those, the utmost caution must be exercised. The appearance of another boat or obstruction can be quite sudden. It is extremely important that the speed of the boat be kept to such a level that it is possible to come to a complete stop within half the distance of visibility.

If your boat is equipped with a fog bell, don't hesitate to use it ... and keep it sounding its signal. Should you hear the bell of another boat, come to an immediate stop and do not attempt to proceed until it is possible to discern its direction and distance. Since it is physically impossible for any one person to see everywhere at once, be sure to ask all the members of your "crew" and any guests you may have aboard to lend you their eyes by acting as lookouts at different vantage points on the boat. If at all practical and possible, it is a good idea to constantly keep track of the boat's position on the nautical chart. If you find that you are lost and do not know your position, do not continue to flounder around blindly. Drop your anchor and wait out the fog until it lifts. You will stand a far better chance of relocating yourself then. But don't forget to keep sounding the fog bell. ●

CHAPTER THIRTEEN

Proper Maintenance and Upkeep

■ A pleasure boat probably represents the second or third most expensive item a person buys, ranking just behind a house, and possibly, an automobile. It all depends on how expensive a car a person buys and how much they spend for a boat. A boat, if properly maintained and looked after, can be a source of great enjoyment and healthful pleasure for many years. Knowing this, it is amazing how many people who own pleasure craft don't care for them properly. It is true that most of them keep their boats appearing clean. But it is of very little or no value to have a boat that is spotless topside but whose basic, routine upkeep of motor and hull has been virtually ignored. There is no question but that getting a boat in proper condition for care-free cruising can be a time-consuming chore. To ease the pain of it a wee bit, just keep one thought uppermost in your mind while you are going about the necessary work ... no matter how much time is expended on making your boat really seaworthy, a lot more time can be spent much more unpleasantly while lying in the water awaiting help.

BEFORE LAUNCHING

As has so often been said, it's truly amazing how fast time goes by and, though it seems like the next boating season is eons away when we put our boats up in the fall, spring is suddenly upon us. For those of us who get started early in fitting out our boats, we are out on the water the day the first warm, spring breezes blow. The others, who whiled away the precious early spring days doing nothing about getting their boats ready, will be on the shore, watching and envying us. If you are among the latter who have waited until warm weather to get started, change your ways and start getting more water-time out of your craft. Get into the habit of fitting out early and, just as important, always be sure your hull is in tip-top condition by starting and keeping a definite program of continued maintenance.

Even if your boat is brand new, there are a few procedures which should be followed before launching. A boat that has been stored over the long, cold winter is most likely to need most or all of the maintenance described below as follows.

Most conscientious boat owners maintain clean hulls by rinsing daily. Salt water skippers pay heed!

HULL MAINTENANCE

The first thing that must be done, in *early* spring, is to take off all of the covering from the boat and let it get a really good airing. There is nothing that will get rid of the musty atmosphere that envelops a boat that has been stored away for any period of time than the blowing of gentle breezes and the rays of sunshine. Not only does this procedure remove unpleasant odors but it helps prevent a dangerous condition from developing. When the temperature rises in enclosed, moist, unventilated areas that are predominantly made of wood, the air-borne spores that cause dry rot become active. That is why it is so important to get the covers off the boat as early as possible and let the air and sunshine dry out any moisture that has formed and also reduce the temperature inside the hull.

Once this simple step has been taken and its mission accomplished, it is time to get to work. The exterior of the hull should be thoroughly scrubbed with a mild detergent and rinsed with fresh, clean water. It's best to do this by working on small areas at a time. Be sure to keep the detergent off any varnished wood because the detergent will cause the varnish to turn white in color. For greater cleaning effectiveness and greater comfort to your hands, use warm water rather than cold. If the place where you are doing this work does not have hot water available from a faucet, buy yourself a fairly inexpensive, immersible electric water heater and, if necessary, a long extension cord. *Voila,* instant hot water and no fear of frostbitten hands.

Any barnacles remaining after this scrubbing are to be scraped off. Make sure that all hull fastenings, such as cleats, are tightly secured. Any that appear to be bent or corroded must be replaced by new ones. The sacrificial zinc anodes, which help to prevent a metal hull from corroding in salt water, should also be replaced at this time. All parts of the steering mechanism must be carefully examined. If necessary, make adjustments. File down any propeller nicks. Above all, do not put your boat into the water until you have made certain that all bilge openings are tightly shut.

The wooden hull, and all other parts of the boat which may be constructed of wood such as deck planks, railings, etc., should be examined for the presence of dry rot. "Dry rot" is actually a misnomer. Dry wood does not rot. The organisms, or air-borne spores, that cause the wood to rot exist only if the wood is saturated with moisture. Rot can occur during the off-season when moisture condenses on the inside of the hull and rainwater wets the outside. The most likely areas for rot to appear are around the transom and behind the moldings. Before caulking and painting a wood hull, replace any planks that show evidence of rot. There is a simple way of checking for the possible existence of dry rot. Using the butt end of a knife handle, cover all woden areas by rapping against the wood. If you get a solid, resounding rat-tat-tat, you can breathe easily because there is no dry rot where you have rapped. Should you get a dull sound coming back to your ears, assume that you have come across dry rot. Turn the knife around and use the blade to poke into the wood across the grain. Should the blade go into the wood easily, and if the wood breaks off and crumbles, your assumptions have been proven correct. You have found dry rot. Dig out all the rotted wood and be certain to properly dispose of all of the residue so that the existing spores can't contaminate any other wooden areas. Then soak all surrounding wood with a wood preservative, many kinds of which are available at marine dealers. This treatment will serve to kill any remaining spores and keep the fungus from spreading while repairs are being made. One method of preventing rot is to apply a liberal coat of linseed oil. The oil does not allow

moisture to collect and penetrate into the wood.

A good practice to follow is to repaint a wood or plywood hull before the beginning of each season. First scrub and then sand the hull thoroughly, after first making sure that the surface is in good shape. Spot paint any bare spots and replace any caulking that is holding badly or appears powdery. Next, apply a fresh coat of marine-grade paint. All work on the boat shouuld be done in a sheltered area. Neither paint nor caulking will adhere very well if the wood contains the slightest amount of moisture.

After several seasons of use, it is best that a wood hull be entirely refinished, instead of constantly applying coat upon coat of paint. To do this, apply a few coats of paint remover to the hull and, when the paint lifts, remove it with a dull-edged putty knife. Following this paint-removing operation, the hull should be scraped with a triangular-bladed boat scraper. Sand the hull until it is completely smoothed out and remove all traces of the old paint. Before caulking, apply a coat of primer. This will allow the filler to get a better hold on the wood. Apply two coats of a good marine-grade paint, sanding lightly after the first coat has completely dried. When the second coat of paint has dried, this job is completed.

When compared to the work necessary to properly maintain a wooden hull, a hull made of aluminum requires very little in the way of proper maintenance. A soap or mild detergent and a soft scrub brush are all the equipment necessary to clean the hull. To preserve the metallic finish, the hull may be waxed, using any one of a number of products which are available for this purpose. If desired, it is permissible to apply a clear lacquer after the hull has been cleaned.

Aluminum has the characteristic of forming a self-protective layer of oxide film which prevents the metal from becoming corroded. Because of this chemical action within itself, aluminum hulls do not require that they be painted. When, somehow, corrosion does occur, it shows itself as small grayish patches of powdery residue. This seeming corrosion in no way harms the hull nor does it affect the efficiency of the hull.

The only reason any boatman can have for ever painting an aluminum hull is to satisfy his (or his wife's) sense of aesthetics. There are quite a number of boat owners who find a hull that is made of aluminum too glaring. Besides which, they like a colorful, distinctive-looking boat that is quickly recognizable as theirs. Nothing wrong with that. All it means is that they will have to do a little more work than the fellow who doesn't mind the silvery glare of natural aluminum.

To paint an aluminum hull, the hull must first be cleaned and rinsed thoroughly. Next, apply a

Bottom-fouling marine growth is rapid in warm waters. Frequent cleaning and application of anti-fouling paint is recommended.

phosphoric acid solution, which will increase the adhesion of the paint to the metal. This solution must be rinsed off with fresh water. Before applying the finishing coat of paint, two grades of primer coats may be needed. One grade can be applied to ordinary surfaces and the second, which is an antifouling primer, is used on the bottom. The antifouling primer helps keep algae and barnacles from forming on the bottom.

Dents and scratches on aluminum hulls can be repaired by using a metallic putty. For use on hulls which have been colorfully painted or built from already-colored aluminum, a putty which has been color-matched can be purchased. The best method for repairing a hull is by means of a double patch. The first step is to cut out a hole larger than the puncture and shape a patch so that it fits exactly into the hole. Rivet a larger patch to the inside of the boat. Then attach the smaller patch from the outside to the larger patch. The use of caulking will serve to seal the area around the patches.

Regular cleaning and waxing of a fiberglass hull will help lessen the effects of dirt grinding into the hull's surface. Under the influence of dirt, the original finish can fade and the smooth surface break down. The thickness of the hull's surface finish, or gel, may, however, fade away. Also, the surface can become scratched and gouged. Spot painting and the use of a matching filler may not be enough to restore the hull's original appearance and the hull will have to be refinished.

To refinish a fiberglass hull, the surface wax must first be removed. This is done by using a wax solvent. The gel coating must also be completely eliminated. It is very difficult to refinish fiberglass without removing the gel as the gel provides a poor adhesive surface for the paint. The gel must be sanded off, rendering the hull rough before it can be painted. Antifouling paint should be applied to the bottom. It is a good idea to repaint the bottom of the hull every year.

ENGINE MAINTENANCE

The basic procedures for readying outboards, inboards, and stern-drives are about the same. The engine manual, which lists maintenance details and specifications, is an invaluable guide for this part of your job. If this manual should be lost, contact the engine's manufacturer and he will generally supply a new one free of any charge. A boatyard mechanic can be commissioned to prepare your engine for the new season, but it is not a difficult process should you want to do it yourself.

Before the start of each boating season, new, properly-gapped spark plugs should be installed. Don't try to cut economic corners by using a set of spark plugs that have been used the previous season. The carburetor can be tuned by adjusting the knobs marked "high speed" and "low speed" or by turning the idle screw. Working with a warm engine, turn the "high speed" knob until the motor sounds as if it is running smoothly. The "low speed" knob and the idle screw are adjusted with the engine idling. Turn the knobs until the motor seems that it is just about to stall. Then turn them slowly in the opposite direction until the motor runs smoothly and quietly.

Carefully inspect all the hoses in the cooling system and replace any that appear to be the slightest bit worn or cracked. A broken hose, or one that leaks even slightly, can overheat the engine. If the leak is allowed to continue unchecked and unrepaired, it can flood the bilge.

Check the boat's engine manual to find out which parts of the engine require lubrication and what type of lubrication to use for the individual parts. On outboards, the lower unit will always require a lubrication change at the start of a new boating season. Remove the two screw plugs on the drive section of the motor and allow the old lubricant to seep out before putting in the new. In addition, a light coating of oil should be placed around the motor clamp screws and the throttle linkage. On inboards and sterndrives, change and replace the crankcase oil and install a new oil filter cartridge. A small amount of oil or grease should be placed in the cups located near the water pump, the distributor, and the generator.

If the motor on your boat is equipped with an electric starter, check the battery charge. Should it be necessary to add water to any of the cells in the battery, be sure to use only distilled water. Inspect the terminals on the battery casing for the appearance of any signs of corrosion. If there is, clean the terminals with diluted ammonia and then give the terminals a coating of grease to prevent further corrosion. Examine the ignition wiring. Replace any wires that show the slightest signs of cracking or fraying.

To prevent corrosion of the outer engine housing, wipe it clean with an oily rag. Retouch any rusty spots or places where the paint is peeling. This will keep rust from spreading. If rust is allowed to go unchecked, it will eventually eat its way through the metal. The final step in this procedure of basic engine maintenance is to tighten all the engine mounting bolts.

DURING THE SEASON

Once you have taken all the steps necessary to get your boat ready to go into the water . . . get it in and have yourself a wonderful time. But don't forget that there are certain chores which must be taken care of during the boating season. Yes, Charlie, there's a price to be paid for all the pleasure you're having.

Upon returning to home base after each day's run, give the boat a good hosing down with fresh, clean water. This will go a long way to preventing salt water from corroding the upper hull. Once in a while, take the extra step of using a mild soap. Keep a sharp lookout for any spots that appear to be worn or wearing and touch them up as soon as they appear.

Proper engine maintenance procedures during the boating season will vary from engine to engine. The engine manufacturer's manual is the best guide to follow and use. As a general guide, the

Before launching, clean fuel system thoroughly. Gummy deposits can be destructive.

crankcase oil usually needs to be drained and replaced with fresh, clean oil after every one hundred hours of use; the oil in the gearbox should be changed after every fifty hours; the spark plugs should be checked after every twenty-five hours. If necessary, clean and regap the plugs. If the spark plug gaps are too small, they will continually foul and thereby rob the engine of power which, in turn, results in wasting costly gasoline. If the spark plug gaps are too large, the engine will be difficult to start, which puts an unnecessary drain on the battery and, again, wastes precious fuel.

At regular intervals during the boating season, make it a habit to go over your boat and remove any and all gear that is no longer of

any use. This will keep the boat from becoming needlessly cluttered.

WINTER STORAGE

There are three storage choices for a boat during the winter months. The most advantageous, probably, is storing the boat in an indoor garage. However, there are mighty few people who are blessed with enough luck, or money, to have a garage large enough to house their boat. The boat must be properly suspended and supported because without sufficient support, the hull can become badly distorted. Of course, even the slightest distortion to the hull is bad. Wooden shelving or placement on horses that can support the weight of the boat should be equal to the task. Never store a wooden boat in a heated garage, should you be one of the lucky ones to have such a storage place. Spending the winter in a heated area will surely cause the wood to dry out to too great an extent, opening its seams.

Most generally, the majority of boats are put to rest for the winter months by being stored in the great outdoors, under a protective canopy. This canopy, which protects the boat from the rain, sleet, and snow of winter, is usually made of canvas. The first thing to do is to build a supportive frame for the covering canvas. Rig a series of A-frames and a ridgepole. These can be made up of ordinary 2x4's which can be purchased at almost any lumber yard. The A-frames can be notched so that they fit tightly against the gunwales of the boat. Run a line through the grommets (around the perimeter of the canvas sheet) and attach it at intervals to the trailer or cradle that is supporting the boat. To allow a fair amount of air to circulate over the boat and give it needed ventilation to prevent the condensation of moisture inside the canvas cover, slit the cover in a few places. Then loosely stitch the edges of the slits together. This will allow enough air to enter and yet not permit any adverse elements entry.

Securing the boat to a slip and then leaving it there for the winter is called putting the boat in wet storage. The boat should be moored in a location that is free from ice. The pressure of ice against the hull of a boat can easily cause the hull to split. Since the boat is to remain afloat in the water for a protracted length of time, it is wise to provide the bottom with a good coat of paint before storing it in this manner. This extra precaution will protect the hull from barnacles and shipworms.

Before putting the boat away in storage, whichever method of storage is used, be sure to open all doors and hatches to ventilate the boat. Remove all excess gear to help prevent the boat from becoming distorted in shape under the excess weight. For obvious reasons, the head (toilet) should be drained and cleaned with an effective disinfectant.

WINTERIZING THE MOTOR

The first step in winterizing the motor is to drain all fuel and water. Allow the motor to run with the fuel line disconnected until it stops. This will burn up any gasoline that may still remain in the carburetor. Empty the fuel tanks and examine them for dirt and rust. If these conditions are present, flush the tanks with kerosene. Water in the tanks can be removed with commercial alcohol. If the cooling system uses salt water, run fresh water into it to wash away any salt deposits. To eject any remaining water, manually turn the starter a few times. To a fresh-water cooled engine, add antifreeze.

Remove the spark plugs, inject a corrosion-inhibitor into the holes, and put back the plugs. For inboards and sterndrives, change the crankcase oil. The internal parts should be coated with oil. Take the top cover off the outboard and spray light oil on all the moving parts. Oil fed into the carburetor on an inboard or sterndrive will distribute the oil over all the moving parts.

Clean all corrosion away from the battery terminals by using distilled ammonia. If necessary, fill the cells of the battery with distilled water. The battery should be stored in a dry place not subject to fluctuations in temperature. Remove the propeller and clean the shaft with sandpaper or steel wool. Then apply a coating of grease and replace the propeller.

Your boat is now ready to rest for the winter. It just awaits the coming of *early* spring when it will once again be treated to your tender, loving care before taking you out for a delightful season of boating. ●

CHAPTER FOURTEEN

Berthing the Boat

■ Over the past several decades, pleasure boating had become so popular a pastime and boating ownership so relatively common, that facilities for servicing and berthing boats became rather hard to find. There just wasn't room enough for the millions of boats that were sold. Those boat owners who were fortunate enough to own waterfront property, were in a position where this problem didn't disturb them at all. In fact, they didn't have to concern themselves with where to berth their boat at the end of a day's cruise. They just parked the boat in their back yard, along their own private dock, and that was that. Also, it was not too serious a problem for the skipper who owned a fairly small outboard that could be trailered from his yard or garage each evening or on the weekend. All he needed was a launching ramp so he could get his boat into the water. Of course, he did run into a degree of inconvenience at times when he looked for a place to land. But, with an outboard of rather small size, he could take the chance of simply nosing his boat into the shoreline near to where his car and trailer were parked. Another slight inconvenience for the trailer-boatman was that there weren't many gas docks around. This problem was over-come by getting gas at filling stations on shore and carrying it in cans. A bit inconvenient but not overwhelming and saved the skipper a few cents per gallon as well. This somewhat made up for the inconvenience. But how about the hundreds of thousands of boat owners who didn't own waterfront property and who couldn't trailer their boats every time they wanted to go out in their own, private craft? There was created a real need for berthing and servicing facilities.

As we all know, very rarely does a real need for something exist that doesn't get fulfilled, eventually. Sooner or later, somebody comes along with enough vision, foresight, intelligence, and finances to recognize that a need exists and does something to satisfy that need. Basically, this is how businesses are born. And that's how the business of providing berthing facilities for the millions of boat owners came into being. A new word was added to the everyday language of millions of Americans ... "marina." It was new, different in a startling sort of way, modern, and so completely satisfied the needs for berthing and servicing of boats that the business became an instant success and spread like the proverbial wildfire.

Marinas satisfy every conceivable need of boat owners throughout the year, in season and out. Naturally located on water, they provide boat owners with docking facilities for their boats as well as many conveniences for themselves. Marinas come in a great variety of sizes, ranging from the small enterprise which features a simple mooring slip for the boat and a hamburger stand for the owner all the way up to the really large, elaborate, almost luxurious layout that has a large number of slips, each one equipped with electrical outlets and running water, a completely stocked marine supply outlet, a fine restaurant and cocktail lounge, and a showroom wherein new boats are on display and on sale. The truly large marinas even feature luxurious shore accommodations in the form of boatels, which are really motels for boat owners whose boats are tied up at one of the slips.

In order for a boat owner to avail himself of dock space at a marina, it is usually necessary for him to sign a contract covering the entire boating season, if not longer. That's why it is well worth the time and effort it takes to do a bit of investigating among marinas before signing on the dotted

line with any one of them. Shop around among several marinas. These are very much the same as any other places of business . . . they differ greatly in size, availability of facilities and conveniences, and in quality of personnel. Not to mention variations in costs. During the boating season, you will be spending a great deal of time at the place where your boat is berthed. It becomes somewhat of your home away from home. So choose your berthing spot carefully. If the enterprise is run in a slip-shod manner, if the services rendered are done so in a slow and sloppy way, and if the prices for less-than-adequate services is excessive, it is easily to become disenchanted with the "pleasures" of boating. However, if you are wise enough to choose a place that is within your financial means and where the service personnel are pleasant and helpful, where the facilities are adequate and maintained well, you will enjoy your boat and boating so much more.

It doesn't take an all-knowing eye to detect a place that is not run in a satisfactory manner. Just look around. You can readily see if the grounds are unkempt; if there aren't a sufficient number of trash receptacles strategically placed in the area; if there's old scraps of wood lying around which will eventually rot and send air-borne spores of dry rot to attack your boat; if the service at the gas dock is slow and discourteous; if there is a lack of desired conveniences such as guest showers, etc. A marina does not have to be luxurious in appearance and

spacious in size; it should be well-maintained and well-run. Most importantly, it should satisfy your needs while fitting your pocketbook. The following suggestions will give you some idea of what to look for when you are going about the business of selecting a marina.

1—Be sure that the marina is a safe place in which to berth your boat. Visit it, if at all possible, under all weather conditions. The entrance should be protected by a breakwater. Otherwise, you may be compelled to enter the narrow berthing channel while being followed by a heavy sea. If your boat has even the slightest tendency to broach, this could cause the boat to crash into a bulkhead. Who needs it? Also, the ideal boat harbor is one that is completely landlocked.

2—One of the best times to visit a marina is during low tide, especially in salt-water areas. There should always be a sufficient amount of water under your boat's keel so that you won't have to worry about being able to leave your slip any time you so desire. There's not much fun to boating if you have to be concerned about being grounded a good deal of the time.

3—One of the most important points to look for is the construction and maintenance of the docks themselves. The pilings must be really secure, the catwalks completely free of any signs of rotting, rusting, and unsteadiness. If the docks don't come up to these standards, don't bother looking at the marina any longer . . . just walk away and look elsewhere.

4—Your need for fueling facilities will depend on the type of fuel your boat uses. Be sure that the servicing dock can supply you with the needed fuel. Regardless of the type of fuel, though, observe how a boat is serviced when it pulls up to the servicing dock. Does an attendant stand ready to catch a thrown line? Is he careful with the filler nozzles and does he wipe up any spillage? Does he help the boat's skipper in getting away? The behavior of servicing personnel is usually a good indication of the quality of a marina. This is an important enough point for you to stay around the servicing dock for a bit of extra time and watch the servicing procedure several times before passing final judgment.

5—Check out the personnel in the rest of the place, especially the boat yard and service departments. This can be done fairly simply by going into the supply store and ask to buy something which is peculiarly marine-like such as a marlinspike or a thimble. An untrained clerk will probably not know what you're talking about and the marine supply store will not be in a position to service you when you need supplies. Check out the quality of the work in the service department and the boat yard. See the yard manager and order some rather incidental work to be done on your boat. Then check it out to see if the

work is satisfactorily done. Also, observe how the men in the yard go about hauling a hull and handling it as they lower it onto a cradle.

6—Another facet of the yard to watch for is the completeness of their service facilities. Be certain that the yard is equipped, in equipment and personnel, to make repairs to your particular hull should the need arise. If you have electronic equipment on board your boat, be sure the yard can service the items that you already have and install others.

7—It is very convenient to be able to store your boat during the off-season in the same area where you dock it during the boating season. Check to see how the yard would handle your boat during the off-season regarding cover frames and proper ventilation; also ask if fire and police protection are offered during the off-season as well as during the season. Even if you are adequately insured against possible losses, it is comforting to know that there is protection.

8—If yours is a sailboat, you should look for a marina that offers the services of someone who can make repairs in sails, as well as in cockpit covers and other canvas. This could be important unless, of course, you are prepared and able to make necessary repairs yourself.

9—A reasonably important point to look for is the availability of electricity and fresh running water at the marina's slips. The availability of electricity would permit you to charge your battery; having fresh running water on hand would make cooking and dishwashing a lot easier and the fresh water tanks on board could be readily filled without using up the time needed to do so at the servicing dock.

10—A great deal of enjoyment is added to the normal pleasures of boating by having certain conveniences on hand at the place where you dock your boat. Among these would be a bath house where showers could be taken by yourself and your guests (most pleasure craft are too small to have their own showers), clean rest rooms, telephones strategically placed along the docks, etc. Also, there should be a parking lot large enough to take care of all the boatowners using a marina. The lot should be marked off in such a manner that you won't find yourself blocked in anytime you want to leave the area.

11—Is there a well-stocked marine supply store at the marina? This could save a lot of time spent in driving all over the area to stock the boat, time that could be put to the more enjoyable undertaking of actually being out on your boat.

The aforementioned are among the more important things to consider when looking around for a marina at which to berth your boat. Depending on your financial and social standing in the boating community, there may be other features which are just as impor-

tant. These would include a fine restaurant, (rather than a hamburger stand), a cocktail lounge, motel accommodations, etc.

It is unlikely that you will find a marina that offers all of the foregoing, especially if your resources are somewhat limited. But it certainly pays big dividends to shop around for the one that will offer you the most of them for the price they charge. One important point to remember is that quality doesn't at all depend on size. A well-run, well-maintained marina which is relatively small in size is much preferred to a big, sprawling type of place which is run in a callous manner and whose personnel are inefficient and sloppy. Don't walk away from a place just because it is modest in size and doesn't offer much in the way of fancy trappings . . . unless size and luxurious facilities are really important to your enjoyment of boating. And don't misunderstand what we are saying. There is absolutely nothing wrong with a place that is large and offers all sorts of fancy facilities . . . as long as it is well-run and staffed by courteous, efficient personnel. A marina of this type, especially if it also offers the facilities of a well-managed social gathering place, can increase the pleasures of boating immeasurably. In most instances, though, a marina which gets that spacious and luxurious generally comes to be known as a yacht club and offers its services on a member-only basis. Membership fees at yacht clubs can run as high as $1,000 per year and more.

In addition to docking slips,

most marinas also provide moorings. These are offshore anchorage points, usually a float or buoy, to which a boat line is attached. Slips are more expensive than moorings . . . and quite justifiably so. They are far more convenient. Loading and unloading, hosing down the boat, and generally coming and going at will are some of the advantages of a slip. To reach a boat at a mooring requires that the boatman be ferried out on a dinghy, usually provided by the marina. Loading a boat from a dinghy, besides being inconvenient, can be a risky business.

A fairly new development in the business of berthing boats is the growth of dry-land marinas for outboard-powered boats. In this type of installation, the boats are stored on cradles or racks on land and lifted out for use by means of a fork lift. Many of these installations offer the usual marina facilities such as winter storage, fueling, maintenance and repair, etc.

Many boatyards that are used primarily for winter storage also offer slip and/or mooring space for rent. Boatyard berthing is less expensive than berthing at a marina slip. However, the services that are available are limited in scope although the usual facilities include bathrooms and provide rowboats with which to reach moorings.

Although there are many offshore moorings which can be rented for as little as only $5.00 for the entire boating season, care must be taken in choosing the site. The ideal place should be free from waves, tidal flows, and stream channels. In addition, it should be sheltered from wind. Of course, provisions have to be made for storing the necessary ferrying equipment, be it rowboat or dinghy, both on and offshore.

Except for the initial expense involved in its purchase, a trailer which is used as a dry-land berthing for an outboard does not add anything to the cost of pleasure boating. Being able to store all the boat's gear as well as the boat itself either in your back yard or in your garage (if it's big enough) goes a long way to overcome the problems of possible vandalism, outright theft, and damage due to the ravages of storm when a boat is berthed in the water.

The most-often used, but not necessarily the best, method of launching a boat from a trailer is the use of a graded, or sloping, piece of equipment known as a ramp. Characteristics of a ramp can come in a wide variety and quality of ramps vary widely. The least important aspect of a ramp is the angle of its slope. Surfaces of ramps may be either concrete or asphalt paving; some are simply made of hard-packed dirt or sand. The important features to watch out for are the extent to which it slopes into the water and the condition of its surface. The angle of its slope, while not a critical consideration, should be steep enough so that the trailer doesn't have to be backed down so far that there is danger of wetting its wheel bearings. Never attempt to launch a boat from a sandy beach without the aid of a ramp. It is quite probable that the wheels of your car will sink into the sand. ●

CHAPTER FIFTEEN

Wind Power

■ There is a certain mystique surrounding the moving across vast expanses of water in a sailboat. A good deal of this is probably due to the mystery concerning one of the most capricious elements in all of nature . . . the wind. Unlike the powered boats which are propelled by a motor which we can dissect, disassemble, study, put together again, and fully get to understand, sailboats are propelled by an element we cannot hold onto or even see. Much like the so-called "common" cold, we know the wind is there but we really don't know how it got there nor where it is going when it leaves. Yet, the wind has been used as a source of power ever since man first put out to sea.

To a far greater degree than motorboating, sailboating calls for acquired, learned skills. This, too, may be part of the mystique of sailing. A man's taming of the wind, putting it to work for his own pleasure and sport, is both a victory of spirit and a compliment to the wonders of nature. People who go sailing are the ones who respond readily to the call of their seafaring ancestors; they are the ones who stand on shore and are thrilled beyond description by the sight of sleek hulls being effortlessly propelled along over the water by beautiful sails which billow in the slightest breeze; they are excited by seeing a sailboat knife through the water, making no more noise than the whispered *swish* of its bow as it cleaves a wave. If you have ever experienced a feeling of unexplainable joy and a quickening of the pulsebeat when you have watched a fleet of sailboats going past, and have as yet never gone sailing, deny yourself no longer. Accept the fact that you were born to be a sailor and give yourself a chance to be a part of this great sport . . . a participant and no longer a mere spectator.

GETTING STARTED

The most important thing to get straight at the very start is to make the proper choice of the sailboat you will purchase. There is a wide variety from which to choose and they come in all price ranges, from the relatively inexpensive 8-foot sailing *pram* to the luxuriously expensive 40-foot *auxiliary.* A thought that warrants much attention is that the enjoyment of sailing does not depend on how much you spend for the boat. If circumstances dictate that your first boat be a modestly-priced affair, don't let that keep you from buying it and getting it out on the water. The main consideration at the point is to go sailing and start acquiring the experience so necessary to the learning of the skills that will make you a better sailor. Even if your first boat is so small that you won't be able to sail more than just a few miles away from your mooring during the first season, you will be gaining valuable experience and knowledge. And the more you know about sailing, the more you will enjoy the sport.

Besides the size of your bank account, there are a number of important factors that must be taken into consideration when choosing a sailboat. You must have a clear picture in your mind of what you want to do with the boat (besides sail it), where you will be using it, and how many people will it have to accommodate. You have to get all your facts assembled and then decide whether you should buy a day sailer, or if a racer or a cruising sailboat would best suit your needs and desires.

TYPES OF SAILBOATS

Day Sailer—This type of boat pretty much fits, or reflects, its name. If what you really want is a boat on which you, your wife, and a couple of kids can go out to enjoy a day of relaxed sailing and be reasonably comfortable while out on the waters, a day sailer is meant for you. Most day sailers are under twenty feet in length, are really pretty easy to handle under sail, relatively simple to maintain in good shape, and don't require that you take out a second mortgage on your house in order to purchase one. With a day sailer, you will spend more time enjoying sailing and less time on its maintenance. Of course, don't plan on any extended sailing adventures in a day sailer. They are not meant for more than a day's excursion . . . out in the morning and back in the evening. If you do fit the description given above, you should select a boat that has a good-sized cockpit and comfortable sitting room. The boat should be of the kind that is easily controlled and is quite stable . . . not one that calls for a crew of nautical acrobats in order for it to stay right side up.

Incidentally, before you decide on what boat to buy, make things a bit easier on yourself by first learning the conditions of the water in your local area, the ones you will most likely be sailing. Don't be ashamed to go around to other sailboat owners who operate in the area and ask them a lot of questions. They appreciate being asked and nothing pleases them more than to be able to talk sailing and sailboats to an interested listener.

The Racing Sailboat—Racing boats are specifically designed to be sailed under strenuous, competitive conditions. They call for a far higher degree of sailing expertise than do the day sailers and

Day sailer; the family fun sailboat.

also require far more expensive and time-consuming maintenance. Everything about a racing sailboat is more complex than a day sailer, such as its sails, rigging, and other gear. As you may have guessed by now, the racing sailboat is not designed for comfort nor is it intended for the purpose of providing the average family with a comfortable day out sailing with the kids.

Most of the racing sailboats under twenty-four feet in length have a centerboard, rather than a keel. The hulls are generally constructed of plywood or fiberglass. Their shapes can vary from flat, round, and V-bottom. Racing sailboats can easily be transported by trailer and launching can be accomplished directly from a beach. The hulls are shallow enough to permit them to be sailed even in waters that are almost shoal.

Invariably, those pilots who reach the upper ranks of racing skippers got their start when they were between the ages of twelve and eighteen. During that time, these youngsters get their basic training by sailing small boats in junior racing events. The training is generally conducted by well-seasoned, experienced teachers. From this junior competition, they graduate to full-sized craft and adult competition. By the time they reach this stage, they are already able sailboat skippers.

Racing sailboats are broken down into one-design classes. Though these may be built by different manufacturers, the same plans and specifications are used. Within a class, therefore, the contest is one of seamanship and skill of the boatman rather than to find out which is the better boat.

There are many, many different one-design classes in racing. The following is only a partial listing of the most popular:

Blue Jay—This is one of the most popular classes of small boats which is used for the basic training of youngsters involved in junior racing. It measures only thirteen and one-half feet in length. The jib and mainsail area is ninety square feet besides the spinnaker it carries. The hull of the boats in the Blue Jay class is made of sheet plywood. Although primarily used in junior racing, there are some areas in the country where there are two divisions in which this class of boat is used . . . junior and senior. A boat in this class, complete with sails, can be purchased for around $700.

Snipe—The Snipe class is the oldest of the one-design classes and has more boats in its class than any other class. The fifteen and one-half feet, V-bottomed hull can be constructed of either plywood, plank, or fiberglass. The total sail area is 108 square feet. Boats in this class are very fast and sensitive. New Snipe class boats cost anywhere from $1,000 to $1,400.

Rebel—Boats in this one-design class are heavily-favored in the Midwestern part of the country. This sixteen-footer has a hull constructed of fiberglass.

Hampton—This sloop runs eighteen feet in length and has found great popularity in the Chesapeake Bay area. Boats in this class are shallow enough to float in about eight inches of water. How's that for sailing in shoal water?

Jet 14—Boats in this class have planing hulls. The Jet 14 is capable of extremely fast speeds. It is an extraordinarily light, two-man boat. Its total sail area is 113 square feet.

Lightning—The Lightning is popular in the International racing-class and offers keen competition wherever it races. Its nineteen-foot length supports a roomy cockpit, it has high initial stability, and is easy to handle. This makes boats in this class highly versatile because they can be sailed as a racer and can also provide a family with all the features of a day sailer. They have 177 square feet of sail area and a planked hull.

International 14—This is a fast fourteen-foot sloop. The planing hull is constructed of molded fiberglass or plywood and features a centerboard.

Star—One of the oldest one-design classes. The Star is strictly a two-man racing boat. Its planked hull measures twenty-three feet.

Thistle—The Thistle can be used for both racing and for family sailing. The boat is seventeen feet long and the hull is made of molded plywood. Its capability of being both a racing and day sailer-type of boat makes the Thistle very popular.

There are many, many more active racing types of sailboats but due to space limitations we cannot list all of them here.

CRUISING SAILBOATS

Sailboats in this class have living accommodations so that with one of these you can plan to spend a weekend or even a month vacationing on one of them. They are also equipped with auxiliary power, either inboard or outboard depending on the overall size of the craft. This is definitely *not* a proper choice as the first boat for a novice to the sport of sailing. Handling a cruising sailboat requires a great deal of prior experience from which one acquires a high degree of seamanship.

The hull of a cruising sailboat is usually made of fiberglass and has built-in flotation devices so that the boat will float if it should capsize. While there are many really large cruising sailboats that are capable of trans-oceanic voyages, recent years have seen a surge in the popularity of boats running twenty-four feet in length and less. One of the reasons for this is probably that these boats can be transported easily by means of a trailer.

Like racing sailboats, cruising sailboats also are built in one-design classes. The following is only a partial list of cruising sailboats that measure twenty-four feet or less in overall length:

Marauder—This is a sixteen-footer that is good for weekend traveling. It is about the smallest and least expensive of the single-class

cruising sailboats. With sails, it costs approximately $1,425. It can easily take on an adult and two children; it has a combination keel and centerboard and can sail in a mere sixteen inches of water.

Corsaire—This is fast becoming one of the most popular of the one-design cruisers. Made in France, it has an eighteen-foot, one-inch waterline, with a good amount of cabin width and headroom. It has an outboard bracket to which an auxiliary motor can be affixed.

Bear—Constructed of wood, this "baby" has an overall length of twenty-three feet, with a waterline of the same length as the Corsaire. It is a good racer and a fine cruiser, designed to withstand the strong breezes and rather rough waters around San Francisco.

Holiday—The twenty-four foot Holiday Junior has two full berths and features an 8 hp Palmer engine. They are easily transported by trailer and most of them can be seen plying the waters off Los Angeles, along Long Island Sound and in Chesapeake Bay.

California—There are actually two boats in this class. One is a twenty-footer and the other measures twenty-four feet. The construction of both of these sizes is fiberglass. The smaller of the two has a keel while the larger has a combination keel and centerboard. Like the Bear, these are well-adapted for use along the West Coast.

There is one thing that all cruising sailboats have in common. All have been designed to provide maximum living accommodations space within their somewhat limited lengths.

PARTS OF THE SAILBOAT

The Rigging—The rigging is the system of ropes and wires that support the mast (standing rigging) and control the movement of the sails (running rigging).

The standing rigging consists of wires called the shrouds and stays. Shrouds support the mast against sideways motion; stays hold the mast in relation to fore-and-aft. Depending on the height of the mast, there can be both an upper and lower shroud. It is of utmost importance that the shrouds be kept taut, but neither too tight nor too loose. If there are two shrouds, both the upper and lower shrouds should have an equal degree of tautness. The stays include the jibstay or headstay, jumper stays, and a permanent backstay. As the wind blows against the sails, the mainsail pushes the mast aft and the jib pulls it forward. In order to get a proper balance between these two forces, the jumper stays, which are attached to the masthead over the jumper strut, offset the forward pulling jibstays. However, the mast as a whole is still being pulled forward by the jib. It is the permanent backstay, which is attached to the masthead and transom, that counteracts this force.

The running rigging includes halyards, sheets, and guys. The halyards are used to raise the sails.

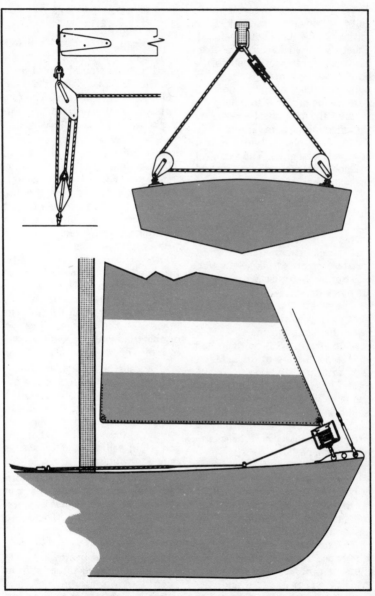

Typical and frequently employed rigs. Top: popular main sheeting rig used on roller reefing boom. Center: fore and aft view of main sheet rig. Bottom: jib roller reefing gear shown in typical installation above decks.

They run up and over the mast, and back down to the deck. Each sail has its own individual halyard. Sheets are used to turn the sails. The main sheet is attached to the boom and runs through a series of pulleys, called blocks. The purpose of the blocks is to relieve the force of the main sheet exerted by the mainsail. There are two jib sheets, only one of which is taut at a particular time. They control the angle of the jib; guys control the spinnaker.

The Sails—Small sailboats have three types of sails: the mainsail, the jib, and the spinnaker. Most sails are made of dacron. Unlike cotton sails, dacron sails will not mildew or rot, shrink when wet, or stretch. In other words, they are more stable.

The mainsail is secured to the mast at three different places: the head, the tack, and the clew. The head is attached to the main halyard and is the top of the sail. The tack attaches the boom to the mast. The clew is at the bottom of the sail. The ideal mainsail shape is like an an airfoil. Battens are flat wood or plastic strips that fit into the mainsail and help preserve its shape.

Unlike the mainsail, which is rounded in shape, the jib is usually cut to a triangular shape. It is raised forward of the mainsail, and its primary function is to funnel wind into the mainsail.

The spinnaker is a large nylon sail shaped somewhat like a parachute. It is designed to catch even the lightest of breezes and, because it can move at right angles to the wind, the spinnaker greatly increases the speed of the boat.

FUNDAMENTALS OF SAILING

The sail sets act as an airfoil, similar to an airplane wing. As the wind passes around the sail, a vacuum is created at the rear, pulling the boat forward. The centerboard or keel, or both, prevents the boat from sliding sideways.

"Two" winds must be taken into consideration while sailing. These are the "true" wind and the "apparent" wind. The true wind is the actual, natural wind whose direction and strength can be felt and measured while the boat is motionless. The direction of the true wind can be seen on a weathervane and its speed can be measured by instruments, such as an anemometer. The apparent wind is that breeze which is felt while the boat is in motion. In other words, it is the modification of the true wind created by your own motion.

The sails on your boat should be trimmed in relation to the apparent wind, which is actually the stronger of the two. This phenomenon is called, in the science of physics, the parallelogram of forces. In sailing, it is known as sailing to windward.

A boat cannot sail directly into the wind. The best angle that can be achieved is 45 degrees off the true wind direction. There are three basic sailing positions: sailing into the wind at a 45-degree angle (known as beating), sailing with wind coming directly from astern (known as running), and sailing at right angles to the wind (known as reaching). Each of these basic sailing positions will be

explained in the following paragraphs.

Beating—In beating, the sails are trimmed in close. In order to sail in a windward direction, a series of maneuvers, called tacking, is required. The boat travels first to one side of the wind, comes about, and then travels on the other side.

Sailing at an angle of less than 45 degrees off the true wind direction results in luffing, or sail flutter, which distorts the ideal airfoil shape of the sail. The common method of getting the right amount of trim is to loosen both the mainsail and the jib until the luff appears. Then tighten the sails until the luff vanishes. Sailing too far off the wind, at an angle greater than 45 degrees, results in sluggish performance.

Since turns are a necessary part of tacking, it is important to know how a sailboat is steered. If the tiller, which is attached to the rudder, is turned toward the left, or port, the boat will travel to the right, or starboard.

Running—Running, or sailing in the same direction as the wind (with the wind astern), is usually easy sailing. The mainsail and the spinnaker are let out and the boat theoretically can travel at the same speed as the wind. The boat's speed will, in this position, be limited only by the friction of the water against the hull.

Running in a strong wind requires a great deal of vigilance on the part of the helmsman (the man at the tiller). He must watch out for waves coming up from astern, which can swing the stern of the boat around. Using the rudder, the helmsman can make corrections for the action of the waves and keep the boat heading downwind.

When running, never allow the wind to slip around to the front of the mainsail. The result can be an accidental jibe, as the mainsail and the boom swing about across the cockpit. Capsizing is then very likely to occur. Always be aware of the wind direction. It is never constant and shifts in wind direction of 20 degrees can take place. Corrective action must be taken immediately when the direction of the wind shifts. This action is taken with the helm to swing the boat with the changing wind.

Reaching—Reaching is sailing at a course which is about 90 degrees to the wind. It is the simplest and the fastest of the sailing positions. Any point between beating and running is reaching. A close reach occurs when the course is less than 90 degrees to the wind. A far reach is more than 90 degrees.

In reaching, the sails are trimmed in the same manner as in beating. They are let out until a luff appears and then trimmed until the luff has vanished.

GLOSSARY OF SAILING TERMS

Sailboating has its own special terminology, in addition to using many of the same terms as other types of boating. The following terms are some of those which are peculiar to sailboating:

Abaft: toward the stern

Abaft the Beam: any direction between the stern and the beam

Abeam: the direction at right angles to the centerline

About Ship: order to tack ship

Abreast: opposite

Alee: the helm is away from the direction of the wind

Athwart: at right angles to the centerline of the boat

Backwind: wind that is deflected from its normal course by the sails

Balloon Jib: large headsail with considerable draft

Bare Poles: no sails set while underway.

Barge: racing term ... to force one's way between another boat and a starting mark

Bear: to approach from windward

Becket: eye in the end of a block to which you may secure a line.

Blanket: to steal wind from the sails of a yacht leeward of you

Bowsprit: spar extending forward of the bow that supports the headsails

Broach to: swinging around to windward in a dangerous manner when running free

Bunt: the middle part of a sail, when furling

Bury: portion of the mast which is below deck

Cat Boat: a single-sailed boat with a mast stepped far forward

Catamaran: a special type of sail

boat which has two hulls joined by crossbeams or a platform

Chain Plates: metal straps to which the shrouds are attached

Close-Hauled: sailing as close to the wind as you are able

Ditty Bag: container for a sailor's sewing kit

Douse: to quickly take in sail

Ease Her: luff a bit

Fair Wind: when the wind is abaft the beam

Falling Off: paying off in a direction away from the wind

Fetch: fetching is when a sailboat arrives at or to windward of a given point when sailing close-hauled

Flatten to: when you trim in the sheets

Flaw: heavy gust of wind

Foot: lower edge of sail

Fore Reach: the headway of a vessel when luffing into the wind

Foresail: the sail set from the foremost of a schooner

Free: to sail when the wind is aft

Full and by: when the course is as close to the wind as possible and all sails are full and drawing

Gaff: spar supporting the head of a fore-and-aft sail

Ghosting: a yacht under headway in no apparent wind

Go About: tacking

Go Adrift: breaking loose

Hard-a-Lee: when the tiller is put hard over, away from the wind

Head Up: luffing

Header: when the wind suddenly shifts towards the bow

Keep Her Full: when ordered to keep the sails drawing wind

Leach: a sail's after edge

Lift: when the wind suddenly shifts away from the bow

Luff: when you shift course more nearly into the wind; also the forward edge of a sail

Mast Coat: canvas sleeve covering the mast at the deck used to prevent water from entering

Mast Step: the wood upon which the mast rests

Miss Stays: failing the attempt to go about

Off the Wind: sailing with sheets slacked off

On the Wind: sailing while close-hauled

Out-Point: sailing closer to the wind than another craft

Pay Off: swinging in a direction away from the wind

Pinching Her: when you sail much too close to the wind

Quarter: the part of a yacht ahead of the stern and behind the shrouds; *off the quarter* is in the direction bearing 45 degrees from dead astern

Reef: reducing sail area

Roach: the curve in the after edge of a sail

Slack away: pay out

Split Tacks: taking the opposite tack while sailing windward of another craft

Stops: pieces of line or canvas used in securing a sail while furling it

Tack: sailing a course with the wind on one side of the yacht; to go about; forward lower corner of a sail

Wind Shadow: the path of dead air on the leeside of a sailing craft

Yawl: two-masted yacht wherein the smaller, after mast is stepped abaft the rudder post

CHAPTER SIXTEEN

Muscle Power

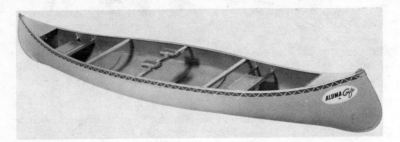

■ In all discussions of boating, the conversation most often is taken up with modern sleek-looking boats that are either powered by mechanized engines or are driven by prevailing winds. Yet, there are times when all that is needed, or can be used because of locale, is a boat that is propelled by the most ancient of all boat--propelling powers ... human muscles.

Rowing and paddling are what we are talking about now. Boats used for these purposes are, of course, of the displacement-hull type. No human being could ever row or paddle fast enough or hard enough to get a boat up to planing speed, so why have a planning hull? Boats known as double-enders (Indian-type canoes are a good example) are best suited for this method of propulsion. Boats with transoms should be designed with fine lines both fore and aft. This will let the boat glide through the water with the least possible amount of friction, thereby reducing the strain on the man

or woman supplying the power.

Obviously, lightness of weight is equal to trimness of design in importance as a factor in making a boat easy to row or paddle. For a boat of this kind, the less frills the better; simplicity is a virtue when making a boat for the purposes of rowing or paddling. And, like virtue, simplicity is a reward unto itself.

There are a number of features about this type of boat that should make it attractive to many water enthusiasts. First of all, there is no problem in getting them launched once you have them at the water site. It takes very little effort and only a few seconds of time. For another thing, their initial cost is well within the budgets of most people and their maintenance requirements are relatively small and inexpensive. Another feature that makes them so attractive and perpetuates their continuing use is the fact that they are so easily transported from home to water or from one water site to another.

Cartoppers are boats which can be hauled around on the roof of the family car and can be taken to wherever it is you want to go. There is absolutely no way of getting into boating less expensively and there is no way of getting into the water any faster than by getting a cartopper. There is no need for rather expensive trailers, winches, lines, ramps, etc. All you need is a simple pair of rack bars on the roof of the car and a couple of normally healthy people with reasonable lifting strength. The people are needed to lift the cartopper to the roof of the car where it is placed on the rack bars. There is no need for any additional equipment except a pair of oars for getting the boat moved through the water. Unless, of course, you prefer and can afford an outboard motor. Even in this instance, the investment is not exhorbitant. All you would need would be a small, one and one-half to three horsepower outboard motor. And this could be taken along in the trunk of the car where it will be in company of all the other boating equipment such as cushions, anchor, and line.

The only specific requirements that a cartopper has to meet is that its beam remain within the limits of the rack bars when being transported; that it be light enough so that two men can lift it easily into position onto the roof of the car (and lift it off easily when the launching site is reached); that it be seaworthy enough for use in protected waters (these boats are not intended for lengthy, offshore cruising); that they have good load-carrying cap-abilities; and that they handle well when launched.

There are a number of types of boats which fit the above description admirably. Canoes are, perhaps, the most ideal and for years we have seen cars travelling down the nation's roads with canoes attached to their roofs. In recent years, though, dinghies have become rather common sights on the roofs of cars belonging to America's increasing number of water buffs.

The most that any boat used for cartopping should weigh is about one hundred and fifty pounds. This keeps them manageable for loading and launching by no more than two men and keeps them from making the car on which they are being transported from becoming top-heavy on the road. The increased use of light-weight aluminum in boat construction has made even flat-bottomed fishing skiffs and V-bottomed outboard utilities (small ones) capable of being used as cartoppers.

Cartoppers can easily be the first step in boat ownership for the man who must watch his budget carefully; it can also be enjoyed by the man who owns a large cruiser already. With a cartopper, the boating season is extended well beyond that enjoyed by the more complex types of vessels. With no elaborate preparations needed to get the boat ready in the spring nor to get it ready for storage in the fall, the owner of a cartopper can take advantage of every bit of favorable weather from early spring right through late fall. ●

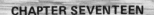

CHAPTER SEVENTEEN

Specialized Craft

■ Besides the boats we have been discussing which were the more or less standard craft which are powered by either mechanical engines, nature's wind, or man's muscle, there are a number of so-called specialty craft that are used as means of water transportation. These don't fall easily into any of the standard categories so they are herewith listed within their own classification as specialties:

INFLATABLES

These are extremely lightweight craft whose hulls are made of inflatable fabric. The hull is made up of quite a number of separate compartments, sealed off from one another, into which air is pumped. This allows them to stay afloat even if a number, or most, of the compartments are somehow deflated. These craft actually squat on the surface of the water and offer very little resistance to the water in the form of friction. If lightly loaded and adequately powered with a small outboard motor, inflatables are capable of achieving a surprisingly high rate of speed. These, as well as the others in the really novelty-class category of water craft, can be most enjoyable.

WATER SCOOTERS

For really great fun in waters

Amphibian: On highway or high water.

that are not too far off-shore, try riding a water scooter. Water scooters can best be described as marine motorcycles. They have handlebars which control the throttle, the same as a land motorcycle. These novelty fun-boats are primarily short-haul in character but they can be fitted with enough power to carry two passengers (including the driver--skipper) and pull two water skiers along behind them.

COLLAPSIBLES

Collapsibles are seaworthy craft that can be unfolded and launched in a matter of only a few minutes. This type of boat is light enough and compact enough so that it can be carried to the actual launching site before it is assembled. A collapsible is capable of taking a small outboard motor which is also easily transported to the water site. This type of craft is economical both in its initial purchase price and as regards its cost of maintenance and continued running.

CANOES

The familiar canoe which all of us have seen and probably have ridden in is not in a true sense a specialized or novelty type of craft. It is a standard type of muscle-powered craft which is light, and narrow of build and is usually propelled by means of hand-held paddles. However, something new has been added to the canoe which probably has The Last of the Mohicans turning in his pad up in the last hunting grounds. There are now canoes on the market which are available

with power. There are models which come equipped with side brackets to which an outboard can be affixed and there are other models which eliminate the side bracket in favor of, would you believe it on a canoe, a square stern.

AMPHIBIANS

An amphibian is a craft that can travel on both water and dry land. Most amphibians are more suited for land and swamp use than they are for water cruising. Much of the power is wasted as an amphibian goes through water and they are extremely slow, travelling about 4 mph.

AIRBOATS

Airboats are propelled along the surface of the water by a large fan mounted at the stern end. They can operate over water, swamp lands, sand, and snow. A model equipped with a 180 horsepower motor can attain a speed of sixty miles-per-hour. These airboats are extremely popular in the Everglades of Florida.

HOVERCRAFT

Hovercraft travel about four inches above the surface of the water on a cushion of air. Over flat land and calm water, they can reach speeds of up to forty miles-per-hour. When the down-thrust engine is turned off, the boat acts as a displacement hull. ●

CHAPTER EIGHTEEN

Safety at Sea

■ While it is true that there are certain hazards inherent to the act of boating, there is no reason why anyone should be hesitant about enjoying the great pleasures offered by boating because of them. All of the dangers involved in boating are things that *might* happen, not things that are certain to happen. There are hazards that might be encountered in the simple act of taking a walk along a neighborhood street. There's always the possibility that you might slip on a piece of apple skin or banana peel, fall down and break some bones or worse; a neighbor's car could go out of control, mount the sidewalk, and strike you down; you might trip on a broken piece of cement with disastrous results. All these and more can happen while taking a leisurely stroll after dinner. But that doesn't stop us from enjoying our evening strolls.

There really is no valid reason for anybody to be afraid of the water or pleasure boating or any other recreational activity . . . nor should anybody approach any of these things with any false sense of security, with no regard to proper safety precautions. If people will take the time and trouble to properly recognize the fact that hazards do exist and that these hazards must be respected as such, then these hazards, to a large extent, will cease to exist as a threat to life and limb. All forms of recreation, including boating, can be enjoyed to the fullest if they will just be approached in a sensible manner.

The application of proper safety measures as they regard recreational boating should in no way detract from the pleasures to be derived from participating in this activity. But, and this is very important, the practice of these measures should never, never be ignored either by the boat owner or his "crew" and guests. The prudent skipper practices safety all the time his boat is in the water and studies it at frequent intervals while he is on shore. He is fully aware of the importance of all federal regulations regarding safety at sea and doesn't look upon them as mere arbitrary rules set down to reduce his enjoyment of his boat. Instead, he looks upon them as requirements that should be thoroughly learned, understood and scrupulously followed so that he and his boating companions can enjoy the pleasure of boating for a much longer period of time than otherwise.

Boating ranks as one of the safest of all the outdoor sports. Yet, accidents do occur. How? It has long been determined, and more than adequately supported by all the evidence at hand, that the greatest majority of accidents take place because of the careless ignorance of those participating in boating rather than the act of boating itself. Carelessly constructed hulls and inadequately manufactured motors do contribute to the boating accident statistics. But irresponsible, downright stupid operation of craft and careless handling of the equipment aboard (or lack of same) is the prime culprit. Most boating accidents that have taken place, and those that will take place, could have been avoided and should never happen. It is true that only a man who is somehow determined to commit suicide will knowingly and willfully jeopardize his own life and the lives of others. Yet, there are many well-intentioned boat skippers who do the very same thing every time they launch their boats. They do this through lack of knowledge which can be corrected by seriously studying, and giving careful thought to, the subject of safety at sea. Knowing how to prevent accidents from happening as well as having a full knowledge of what to do when an accident does occur, can and will result in a tremendous reduction in the number of problems that can be encountered while on the water.

Some of the hazards, or accidents, which can be encountered while out savoring the joys of boating are fire, explosion, collision, and running aground. These can result in the boat capsizing or sinking, or in people drowning, being seriously burned, etc. We again state that most of these are caused by irresponsible operation of the boat by irresponsible skippers. Not bothering to learn the rules of the watery road, not knowing the significance of buoy markers, loading a boat beyond its capacity, operating a boat while under the influence of alcohol, not seeing to it that the boat is equipped with sufficient and efficient safety devices . . . these are all acts of irresponsibility that can, and usually do, result in accidents, accidents which can cause serious or tragic bodily injury and damage to the property of others.

Safety at sea is a subject which is so broad in context that it encompasses virtually all aspects of boating. It concerns itself with the construction of hulls, the design and function of power equipment, the maintenance and upkeep of boats, boat handling, and many other specific subjects which have been individually covered in previous chapters. Therefore, there will undoubtedly be much in this chapter that will be a repeat of what you may have read in other chapters. And that is as it should be. Safety measures and their application are so vital to the enjoyment of boating that they bear much repetition. Remember one basic fact and keep it uppermost in your mind: there is no way of walking away from an accident at sea.

ORGANIZATIONS CONCERNED WITH SAFETY

Several public organizations devote themselves to the promotion of safety as it affects pleasure boating. They are known as public organizations because they are not agencies of the federal government or any other governmental body. The best-known of these volunteer organizations are:

UNITED STATES POWER SQUADRONS

This is a volunteer organization of over 82,000 members who are active in over 390 local Squadrons. There are units in areas throughout the United States as well as in several areas around the world. These squadrons make available, to any who are interested, educational programs covering basic boating safety and piloting. There are more advanced courses which are available only to those who are so devoted to recreational boating that they join the Squadrons as members. The entire organization is a non-profit, self-sustaining, private membership body that is dedicated to the teaching of better and safer boating.

Inquiries regarding local squadrons and/or when and where boatmen can avail themselves of free classes in boating instruction should be addressed to: USPS Headquarters, P.O. Box 345, Montvale, N.J. 07645.

UNITED STATES COAST GUARD AUXILIARY

This, too, is a voluntary organization made up of civilians who own boats, private airplanes, and amateur radio stations. Although it is a strictly non-military group, it is administered by the United States Coast Guard. Its only mis-sion and purpose for existence is the promotion of safety in small craft operation and they carry out their mission through educational courses, boat examinations, and operational activities.

A very well-known program of the Auxiliary is the one which conducts Courtesy Motorboat Examinations. At the request of a boat owner, the Auxiliary will send a team of specially-trained members to conduct a thorough check of his boat. Note: the examination is conducted only at the request of the boat owner. There is no compulsion to subject a boat to this examination but a wise skipper will not pass up this opportunity. Boats that fail to meet the Auxiliary's strict set of requirements are not reported to any authorities; instead, the boat owner is urged to have any defects they may find corrected and to request a reexamination. Boats that do meet the inspecting team's requirements, qualify for the award of a distinguishing decal. More importantly, the boat owner whose boat qualifies for this decal knows that he is operating a well-equipped, safe craft that will permit him to enjoy all the pleasures of boating without fear or encountering any hazards due to faulty hull construction or engine malfunction.

AMERICAN NATIONAL RED CROSS

This very well-known organization offers programs in water safety in areas all over the country. It consists of over 3,000 local chapters and all of them are involved in the teaching of swimming and related water safety skills. The Red Cross also sponsors a program in small craft safety which includes courses in canoeing, rowboating, outboard boating, and sailing.

One of the most important services rendered to the public by the American Red Cross is its courses in first aid training. Any boat owner who has a real, honest concern for his own welfare and the welfare of his family and boating guests should learn what to do in the event of bleeding, fractures, stoppage of breathing, shock, burns, and other fairly common personal emergencies.

The Red Cross publishes a wide variety of safety pamphlets and posters as well as textbooks which are used in the training programs which it sponsors. It also produces a number of excellent informational and instructional films. The films are usually available on a loan basis free of charge to interested groups and publications are for sale at a very nominal fee. For information regarding these and all other matters concerning the activities of the American Red Cross, contact the chapter in your local area. It's listed in the phone book.

SAFETY IN CONSTRUCTION

Hulls—Logically and practically speaking, safety at sea begins with the design and construction of the boat itself. When buying a brand new boat, the purchaser should make sure that the boat he is contemplating buying is built by a reputable manufacturer. There are too many sound, seaworthy boats that are honestly built and constructed to proven designs for the boat-buyer to get stuck on some freak of questionable worth.

If you're in the market for a used boat, give serious consideration to enlisting the services of a qualified marine surveyor. He is well worth the price of his hire. He has the expertise to appraise the condition of the hull, the engine, and other equipment on board. Don't let your own enthusiasm for a boat keep you from hiring someone who might well find defects that you could never see. Getting the boat thoroughly inspected by an impartial surveyor is a sound investment.

Deck Safety—Any boat which is in Class 1 or larger will probably have side decks which permit persons to move fore and aft and back again. It is essential that these decks be wide enough so that a person's feet can be placed fully on them, even if the available area means they have to walk sideways. Also, most deck materials get slippery when they are wet (it is practically impossible to keep a deck dry). Therefore, it is most imperative that anti-slip protection be provided at all critical points. Fiberglass decks can be roughed up to achieve antislip protection; there are materials for this purpose which can be added to deck paints; there are special anti-slip strips which can be attached to the deck by means of self-adhering backs. Anti-slip protection should be added to any area where a person can or has slipped, even if such slippage happened only once.

A third point in providing safety on a boat's deck is that there must be an adequate number of hand-holds. These are places where someone walking on deck can grab and hold onto should it be necessary that he do so. These hand-holds should be sufficient in number and so spaced that one is never out of the reach of someone moving forward and aft, or when coming aboard or leaving the boat. A good way of practicing safety at sea is never to move about a boat without holding onto something that is strong enough to bear your weight.

Still another area of deck safety for personnel that should not be overlooked concerns lifelines. These are sometimes referred to a liferails. Whatever you may call them, if your boat is large enough for them, don't be without them. They can be used to completely enclose a deck by being carried forward from the side rails to join the low metal rails (known as pulpits) at the bow and stern.

ENGINE AND FUEL SYSTEM SAFETY

Just mention the subject of safety at sea to any boatman and the first thought that comes to his mind is the prevention of fire and explosion. These are the most serious and most dramatic (as well as traumatic) hazards connected with boating. More people stay away from boats because of a fear of fire and/or explosion than any other phobia in the books. Fire, when it does occur, generally originates in either the engine room or in the galley. Improper

equipment, faulty installation, or careless operation of the equipment is usually the direct cause of a shipboard fire. And every one of these causes need never be present. Each of them is under the direct control of the boat owner.

Engines—Engines must be compatible to the hulls which respond to their power. Care must be taken to avoid extremes of either underpowering or overpowering. Both are equally bad medicine. A naval architect, or someone equally familiar with this phase of boat design, should be consulted when the first engine is originally installed and any time there are any subsequent changes made.

Under no circumstances are automobile engines to be used for marine duty and that includes those that may have been converted by amateur mechanics. There are basic differences between automobile engines and marine engines including differences in the methods of lubricating and cooling them. To use an automobile engine on a boat is an invitation to a whole bag full of troubles. Either use an acceptable type of engine which has been designed specifically for marine use or get a converted automobile engine that has been produced by a commercial, professional engine-converting organization.

Besides using the proper engine for the job at hand, make sure that it is installed properly. If it isn't, you'll literally be sitting or standing on a keg of dynamite, the fuse already lighted. It will be resting there below the deck under your feet, just waiting to blow you and all around you to Kingdom come. An improperly installed engine can easily drip gasoline into the bilge where it will mix with air to form an explosive combination. All it needs is a slight spark to set it off ... with tremendous effect. The vapors from just one cupful of gasoline have the explosive power of about fifteen sticks of dynamite ... enough to completely destroy a large motorboat.

FUEL SYSTEMS

Fuel system safety is primarily concerned with the prevention of fires and explosion. However, don't overlook the reliability aspects of the system. No matter how fireproof and explosion-proof the system may be it is of little value unless it ensures a continuous flow of clean fuel to the engine.

Carburetors—These should be of an approved marine type, equipped with flame arresters as protection against backfire. Those of updraft design should have a pan which is covered with a fine mesh screen attached under the carburetor which is there to collect any drip. By running a copper tube from the bottom of the pan to the intake manifold, any leakage will be sucked back into the engine and will not be a source of any possible trouble. The more modern downdraft designs feature an air intake that is turned upward at about a 45 degree angle, providing a natural residue chamber for the collection of drippings. Regardless of the design, though, flame arrestors must be installed and kept clean to protect against

fire and explosions which could otherwise be caused by backfire.

Fuel Tanks—This is one place where one should not even attempt to economize. Fuel tanks should be well constructed and should be installed in such a manner that they are permanently secured against moving about once underway. If this is not done properly, you are running the risk of having one of them come apart under the pressure of pitching about and rolling which are natural to a boat at sea. What happens then does not present a pretty picture. The whole bilge becomes full of vaporizing gasoline. In the unlikely event that you haven't already taken off like a rocket when you discover what has happened, all you can do is immediately shut off the engines (no point in pressing your luck as far as sparks are concerned) and all other electrical equipment, get the fuel completely diluted with water and then use your hand pump and muscle power to get the mess out of the bilge. Keep pumping until the bilge is completely cleaned out, meanwhile getting as much air ventilation down there as is possible. Once the liquid is completely pumped out, let the bilge air out as thoroughly as possible before you attempt to use any of the electrical equipment on board. Then and only then, can you get to work on your ship-to-shore radio-telephone to seek help. Do you think it worthwhile to make sure that the fuel tanks are properly installed and secured? You bet your "life" it is!

Fuel Filler Pipes and Vents—Connections between the gasoline tank and the filling plate on deck must be completely tight. Also, it is essential that the fuel fill be in such a location that any leakage or spillage will go overboard, not inside the hull. Each tank should be equipped with a suitable vent pipe that leads outside the hull; never allow vent pipes to terminate in any closed spaces.

Fuel Lines—These should be made of seamless copper tubing and as much of them should be within clear sight as possible to permit easy inspection. They must be protected from any possible damage. Soft, non-ferrous metal clips with rounded edges should be used to secure them against vibrating.

Fuel Pumps and Filters—If electric fuel pumps are used, they should be located at the engine end of all fuel lines. They should only be able to operate when the ignition switch is "on" and the engine is actually turning over.

Fuel lines should have filters which are installed inside the engine compartment. Filters should be supported in such a manner that their weight is not borne by the tubing of the fuel line.

It is of utmost importance that all fill pipes and tanks be bonded to the common ground. Also, it is a matter of law that tanks must be separated from living quarters by bulkheads.

FUEL

The greatest single danger to lives and property aboard ship is

... explosion. Nothing else can so completely destroy a ship and all that is within its confines ... and do it so quickly. If the explosion itself doesn't do the complete job, the fire which usually follows an explosion finishes it off. And the single, greatest, most frequent cause of explosion is the fuel which is used more than any other for boats in the pleasure class ... gasoline.

The volatile characteristics of gasoline are pretty fantastic. As mentioned a bit earlier, the fumes from just one measly cupful of gasoline can create enough explosive force to equal that of fifteen sticks of dynamite. Treat gasoline with all the tender loving care within you. The National Fire Protection Association states, "There are few other uses of petroleum products by the public in which the fire and explosion hazards parallel those possible in a motor craft."

Because of its explosive nature, gasoline should have very limited use on board a boat. And other equipment and gear which is brought on board should be chosen in consideration of the gasoline that must be used, such as fuel. For this reason, and because it is strictly forbidden by Coast Guard regulation, don't ever use a gasoline stove on board a boat. These are meant for use only on shore and shouldn't even be brought on board. They just have no place on a boat.

Nor should any portable charcoal grills be used on the deck or anywhere else on a boat. They are great at picnics and in your backyard, but can prove deadly at sea.

A portable grill can easily be upset by a rolling sea or by the wake of a passing boat. This could cause a glowing chunk of coal to be dumped into the boat. If you're really lucky, you will escape experiencing an explosion. But you're almost certain to find yourself fighting a fire. It's alright to carry one of these grills along if you are heading for a boating campsite and are planning a barbecue picnic. But don't use it on board.

What should you use in the galley for cooking, etc.? Have an approved kerosene, alcohol, or solid fuel stove installed according to approved, proper standards; keep the galley clean and free from all unnecessary clutter because the cleaner the galley the less chance there is for a fire to get started and the easier it is to extinguish if one should get started; make sure the galley area is well ventilated; and use only non-combustible materials for curtains, drapes, etc.

SAFETY IN OPERATIONS

There is no aspect of the operation of a boat that doesn't somehow or other concern itself with the subject and practice of safety at sea. The art of boat handling, which we discussed to some extent in Chapter Eight is replete with situations calling for proper safety measures; in Chapter Nine we covered the Rules of the Road which are really guidelines to safety in piloting a boat; and so it goes almost through the entire subject of boating. There just is no separating the practice of boating from the practice of safety. In this section, we will touch on some aspects of safety opeation of a boat that have not been discussed before, and we will repeat some others.

Fueling—As noted earlier, gasoline is a most volatile, explosive element and must be handled with extreme caution. For this reason, fueling must be one of the most careful, methodical tasks performed on a boat. Unfortunately, it is sometimes done in a careless, sloppy manner and this invariably leads to a dangerous situation, if not to actual tragedy. The following is presented as a checklist and should be religiously adhered to every time a boat is fueled.

Before Fueling

1—Make sure that all cigarettes, cigars, pipes, etc. are out.

2—All equipment capable of producing a spark must be turned off.

3—Close all hatches, doors, and windows.

4—mooring lines must hold boat securely tied to dock, without slack.

5—have a fire extinguisher ready and handy.

While Fueling

1—Ground the fuel nozzle by putting it in contact with the engine intake pipe.

2—Be careful to avoid the spilling of any fuel.

After Fueling

1—If, despite great care, some fuel has spilled, wipe up or hose down the deck.

2—Open all hatches, doors, and windows to aid ventilation.

3—After about five minutes of ventilating the boat, make a physical check for any lingering gasoline fumes. By physical, we mean use your nose. There is no better detecting device for gas fumes.

4—You may start the engine only after feeling absolutely sure that no gasoline fumes are present.

5—Maintain the fuel system according to the manufacturers' recommendations and inspect it periodically. It is amazing what a well-trained individual can tell at a glance. For example, if the fuel line fittings feel damp, it generally means that gasoline is escaping and evaporating.

Capacity plate: Water weight-watcher.

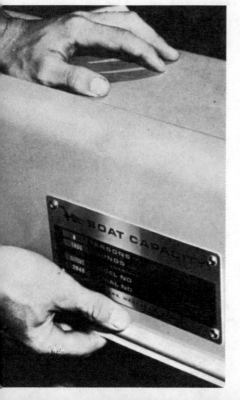

LOADING THE BOAT

It is highly dangerous to overload a boat with passengers or gear. Many boat manufacturers now install a capacity plate showing the recommended weight capacity both in terms of number of people and total weight. Total weight means just that ... the combined weight of all passengers, motor, fuel, and equipment. These capacity values are recommended for fair weather boating. Adjustments should be made if there is any likelihood of running into foul weather and rough seas. Do not be foolhardy enough to ignore the manufacturer's recommendations. They have fully tested their boat and have a much better knowledge of the boat's limitations than you do.

If the boat is not equipped with a manufacturer's capacity plate, the total weight a boat can safely carry can be roughly calculated by using a simple formula. Multiply the overall length of the boat, its maximum width, and its minimum effective depth by 7.5. The resulting answer will give you some idea of the total carrying capacity of the boat in pounds.

Weather and water conditions must always be taken into consideration. If the water is rough, the number of recommended passengers and the total weight must be reduced. Better still, if the water is really rough, don't go out.

Don't forget, too, that there is a maximum horsepower load that can safely be put on an outboard. This is as much a factor in considering the capacity of an outboard as are the number of passengers and the total weight. See previous guideline chart.

BOARDING A BOAT

As in the performance of almost any physical task, there is a safe way and an unsafe way in which to board a small boat. Always step into a boat as close as possible to its center, while keeping the body low. If boarding from a beach, come in over the bow while somebody else holds the boat steady. Never, never jump into a boat or use the gunwale (edge of the boat's hull) as a step. Never carry any gear or equipment with you as you are boarding a boat. File the stuff nearby on the dock so it can be reached once you are in the boat. Better still, have somebody hand it to you.

WATER SAFETY

Before anybody goes out boating, whether as a skipper or a passenger, he should know how to take care of himself should he find himself unceremoniously dumped into the water because of some emergency on board the boat or because he has slipped from the deck. The most fundamental, basic aspect of this ability to care for one's self is to know how to swim. Then follows the acquiring of the knowledge of how to properly use the life saving devices on board and what to do if you should suddenly take an emergency dunking. Most swimming is, of course, larned in well-maintained, warm pools where safety and rest are easily available

only a few feet away from the swimmer. It behooves all skippers to see to it that he and his "crew" practice survival under adverse conditions periodically. This would include "abandon ship" drills and actually going into the water from the boat in simulated emergency drills.

More than any lectures or other methods, these drills will impress upon people the absolute necessity for having their life saving devices readily accessible and in good condition. It is equally necessary to know how to properly use life jackets, life vests, etc. A good place to start the serious study of water safety might well be the lifesaving and swimming classes given at your local "Y" or community recreation center.

As mentioned earlier in this book, the life jacket provides the greatest degree of safety among life saving devices. But to do anybody any good, they should be stored in several locations on board so that people won't be cut off from them in the event of fire or other emergency. They must be readily available or else a boat might just as well be without them for all the good they will do. It is most important that the skipper of the boat order everybody into their life jackets the moment he is aware that an emergency might be arising, rather than wait for that moment of near panic when the emergency actually strikes. No matter how bulky and uncomfortable they may be, it is better to put them on and wear them than to find yourself in the cold water without them. For safety's sake, they should be worn

Board boat as close to center as possible; stem-to-stern, port-to-starboard.

at all times by all non-swimmers, children, and persons who may be physically handicapped. These are the people who are most likely to panic and become totally helpless should an emergency strike suddenly. Should the boat be out cruising at night, it should be standard operating procedure that all persons on deck after dark wear their life jackets.

It is a good idea for the skipper and his regular "crew" to practice donning their life jackets in total darkness. This can easily be done by simply putting on blindfolds while getting into the jackets. Of course, the life jackets should be inspected periodically to make sure they are always in good condition. They should be tried on from time to time to make sure all the straps and fittings are not unduly worn or frayed.

While buoyant cushions are fine when used as something to hold onto while in the water, they should never be worn on a person's back.

IN CASE OF EMERGENCY

Despite all the safety measures and precautions that are properly taken, accidents can and do occur. When this happens, the primary thing to remember is DO NOT PANIC. In most cases, bodily injury and damage to property can be kept to a minimum if the right action is immediately taken.

ACCIDENTS

Boat accidents involve personal injury and property damage due to collision between two vessels, flood, fire, explosion, grounding, etc. The law requires that any boat owner involved in a collision with another vessel stop his craft immediately and render all assistance possible. He must also identify himself and his boat to the other party. However, the law is also firm on the point that the assistance he renders be limited by the fact the he should in no way further endanger himself or his craft. All boats in the vicinity of an accident are not to leave the scene and should render all possible assistance.

The owner of a boat which is involved in an accident involving another boat must submit a written report concerning the accident within a specified period of time. This report is submitted either to the United States Coast Guard or to the proper authority in the

state in which the boat is registered. In the event there is a loss of life due to the accident, the report must be filed within forty-eight hours after the accident. If there is serious bodily injury other than a fatality, or if there is damage to property exceeding $100, the report is to be submitted within five days. It is always best to file a report as quickly as possible unless it is absolutely clear that the accident is so minor that there couldn't possibly be $100 worth of damage and there is absolute certainty that no one was injured. Failure to file a report in the event of a reportable accident can result in severe penalties.

DISTRESS SIGNALS

There are many ways of communicating distress to another boat or to the United States Coast Guard. A flag or ensign being flown in an upside down position, a white cloth flying from the highest point on the boat, the rapid sounding of a horn, bell, or whistle are all common signals that can be easily noticed by another boat. Recently, the Coast Guard inaugurated a new distress signal for small boats, ones that are not equipped with electronic signalling devices and who do not carry signal flags. A boat owner in distress should stand where he can clearly be seen by a passing boat and slowly raise his outstretched arms above his head and slowly lower them in a continuous motion.

Should a boat owner find himself in distress during the night or other periods of poor visibility, he can summon help by sending the international morse code signal SOS (3 dots, 3 dashes, 3 dots sent as one group of letters, with no hesitation between each letter). This signal can be transmitted over the boat's radio and/or with the boat's spotlight. Also, there are flare signals that can be used. Any boat in the area of another boat seen sending these signals should respond to the call for help immediately and render all assistance possible.

The Coast Guard can be contacted by radio-telephone via 2182 kc. All Coast Guard rescue stations, marine operators, and many boat operators maintain a constant vigil on this frequency. If in grave or immediate danger, the call for help should be preceded by the word "MAYDAY" exclaimed three times in rapid succession. The sender of any such distress signal should be ready to supply the following information:

1—The sending boat's name and radio call letters.
2—The sending vessel's position in latitude and longitude or true bearing and distance in nautical miles from a widely-known geographical point.
3—Nature of the distress or difficulty.
4—The kind of assistance required or desired.
5—The number of persons aboard and the condition of any who may be injured and the extent of their injuries.
6—Whether the vessel is in immediate danger of sinking or capsizing.
7—A description of the boat, including type and length, color

of hull and design of its superstructure.
8—The boat radio's listening frequency.

FIRE

Next to explosion, fire is the greatest single danger facing the boat owner and those on board his boat. We have previously discussed the fire prevention steps that should be taken while fueling the craft. We have also discussed fire-fighting equipment which must be kept on board under federal regulations . . . but we will repeat them here. Every boat must, and should, be equipped with an adequate number of suitable fire extinguishers and should also carry several pails or buckets. All fire extinguishers should be checked periodically to see whether their pressure is up to standard requirements. All cracked or broken hoses should be immediately replaced. Fire extinguishers and buckets should be easily accessible. All adults on board should know where extinguishers are stored and be fully familiar with their operation.

A fire above decks should be approached from upwind, allowing the breeze to carry the extinguishing substance into the flames. This will also help keep smoke and noxious fumes from blowing into your face and up your nostrils. Also, the boat should be brought to a complete stop, if possible, as soon as there is an outbreak of fire. This will help keep the flames from being fanned by the apparent wind. Try to keep the fire downwind from the rest of the boat to keep it from spreading. If the fire is toward the stern, turn the bow into the wind; if the fire is forward, turn the stern to the wind. A fire can be smothered by wetting a blanket or other large piece of cloth and tossing it on top of the flame. This works just fine if the fire is very small and localized. If the burning object is moveable, toss is over the side, being careful to use asbestos gloves or other suitable equipment so that your hands don't get burned to a crisp.

A fire below decks or in the engine compartment is a much more serious matter. Close all doors, windows, and hatches in an attempt to rob the fire of oxygen. Gasoline is highly flammable and explosive. In case of an engine fire, immediately turn off the fuel supply. To prevent the fuel tanks from getting hot and vaporizing the gasoline into explosive fumes, continually wet the tanks until they are about the same temperature as the outside air.

LEAKING HULL

A leaking hull can be the direct result of a collision with submerged or floating objects, or with another vessel. Minor leaks are usually due to the opening of a hull seam or the failure of a fitting or hose. Unless there is a major hole in the hull, the craft can be saved and kept afloat by quick action.

Standard equipment on any boat should include either an electric or a hand pump. But even if your boat is equipped with an electric pump, it would be pru-

dent to have a hand pump along just in case there is a power failure. At the first sign of a leak, start the pump doing its thing and immediately head for shore. Have all passengers don their life jackets.

Frequently, the leak can be easily located. However, do not hesitate even a moment to rip up the floorboards to find the hole that is the cause of the leakage. When the leak is found, stuff anything available into the hole in order to stem the flow. A piece of plywood, tin, or canvas should then be nailed over the plug. Sure, this plug and cover will not be perfectly watertight, but it will help gain time.

If the boat is rammed by another, stop immediately. It may be necessary to travel in reverse if the bow is damaged. This will help reduce the intake of water and will make repair work easier.

A damaged fitting or hose is also a cause of leaks. Since the hole is usually circular in shape, a wooden plug can be used. Frequently, the water intake hose for the engine is damaged or split. A spare hose can be attached to the engine and run back through the original hole. Obviously, spare hoses of all kinds should be part of your boat's basic equipment.

MAN OVERBOARD

Even if the person who goes overboard into the drink is a good swimmer, speed is of the essence in rescuing someone who has fallen from a boat. The stern of the boat should be immediately turned away from the immersed individual and the engine stopped so that there is a reduction in the chance of the person being caught in the whirling blades of the propeller. Next throw him a life preserver. This can be in the form of either a life ring or a buoyant cushion. While keeping the man in clear sight, start up the engine again and maneuver the boat so as to approach him from downwind. If there are high waves, an upwind approach may cause you to lose sight of the man in the water. When you've gotten close enough to where you can assist the man back into the boat, shut the engine once again. Always help the man board the boat at its most stable point, either the bow or the stern. Trying to pull him aboard over the sides may cause the boat to tip or capsize.

In the preceding illustration, it is an adult man that has fallen overboard. Unfortunately, more often than not it actually is a child who goes into the water. That is why the prudent skipper always insists that all children on board his craft always wear their life jackets. A child is less well-equipped physically to stay afloat without the aid of a lifesaving device than is a grown man. The life jacket will help keep a child afloat while the boat is being maneuvered into position to affect the rescue.

ABANDONING SHIP

Most boats, even if gutted by a fire, will stay afloat quite a while. Always stay in the vicinity of the ship after having obeyed the order of the skipper to abandon ship. It is far easier for those coming to help you to spot a hulk of a ship

in the water than it is to sight a person swimming. Also, remember that visibility over water is usually quite good. You might very well be deceived by the land that appears to be well within your ability to swim. It may very easily be beyond your capability.

Before abandoning ship, send out whatever distress signals you can possibly get off. However, when it is time to jump . . . jump. It is fervently hoped that long before jumping, all passengers would have put on their life jackets.

EMERGENCY FIRST AID

Common sense dictates that every boat should be equipped with an easily accessible first-aid kit. The kit should be adequately

Add any special items required to prepackaged first-aid kit.

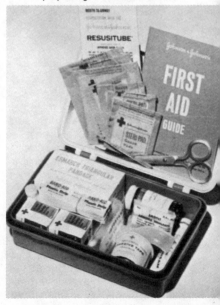

stocked with enough items so that, if necessary, it could be used to treat all the passengers who might be on board. Each and every person on board should be aware of the location of the first aid kit.

First aid equipment should be packaged in a container that cannot rust nor should it be capable of absorbing moisture. In other words, neither metal nor cardboard should be used for storing first aid supplies. Rather, a plastic box such as is used for carrying fishing tackle or tools should be employed for this purpose. While it should have a tight-fitting, moisture-proof cover, it should never be locked. There is no point in having a first aid kit that isn't readily available for use at the moment there is an emergency.

A properly equipped first aid kit contains a certain number of instruments and surgical supplies as well as a number of consumable supplies. The following is a fairly representable list of contents which should be carried in a first aid kit, regardless of the size of the boat:

1—A pair of small, sharp scissors. If there is room for two pair, the second pair should be of the blunt-end surgical type. It is well to also have a pack of single-edged razor blades along.

2—A number of safety pins of assorted sizes.

3—A pair of small, pointed eyebrow tweezers. The tips must meet perfectly to pick up small objects and to be able to pull splinters out of fingers.

4—An inexpensive oral and/or rectal type of thermometer.

5—A small, metal eye-washing cup.

6—A tourniquet which is to be used only, repeat, only in case of bleeding that absolutely cannot be controlled by using a compress.

7—It is amazing how much pain can be eased by the application of heat or cold. Take along a hot water bottle and an ice bag, or a combination if there isn't enough room for separate items.

8—Any adequately equipped first aid kit will include a resuscitation device such as a Cross Venti-breather.

9—An adequate supply of sterile gauze bandages, in a variety of sizes. Take along varied-sized squares that are individually wrapped as well as bandage rolls of varied widths. There should also be at least one 40" triangular bandage which can be used as a sling or as a major compress. Elastic bandages come in handy in the event of sprains or if splints have to be used.

10—Assorted sizes of waterproof adhesive tape.

11—Plenty of absorbent cotton in standard size rolls.

12—Individual cotton-tipped swabs for applying antiseptics and for removing foreign substances in cuts, eyes, and/or ears.

13—A supply of antiseptic liquid such as iodine or merthiolate in individual crushable ampoule applicators.

14—A tube of white petroleum jelly. Be sure it is the plain variety, not the carbolated. This comes in handy for the treatment of small burns.

15—A tube of antiseptic ointment to use on general cuts, abrasions, and infections of the skin.

16—Aspirin or any other related compound to be used as an ordinary pain killer. Might be a good idea to also take along something stronger such as codein tablets for more severe pain.

17—Crushable ampoules of ammonia inhalants come in handy to relieve symptoms of faintness or dizziness.

18—One of the most often used items is a remedy for seasickness. Yet, these are most often effective only if taken before embarking. Once nausea causes a physical reaction, forget it. Nothing helps.

19—There are other items which can be taken along such as laxatives, anti-diarrhea drugs, antihistamines, etc., etc., etc. Use your experience and the advice of a physician to complete the items in your first aid kit. The number of each of the items will depend to a great degree on the size of your boat and the number of passengers you generally have aboard. However, the one major item you won't want to overlook, because it makes all the other items more workable and more worthwhile, is a good first aid manual. One of the best available anywhere is the *First-Aid Textbook* published by the American Red Cross.

Of course, there may be other items which you will need to add to the kit because of the area in which you will be cruising. For example, if you will be cruising and possible swimming in areas that are noted for the presence of poisonous water snakes, better take along a reliable snakebite kit.

ARTIFICIAL RESPIRATION

If caught in time, it is possible to revive someone who has stopped breathing. Mouth-to-mouth respiration is probably the best way to effect a revival. A plastic resuscitator tube can be used instead of direct contact. Artificial respiration should be given for at least four hours. Frequently, the recovery is only temporary and the patient should be closely watched for a relapse. The following steps are for mouth-to-mouth respiration:

1—Loosen the clothing and put a blanket over the victim.

2—Check to see if the mouth is blocked. Remove anything, such as chewing gum or mucus.

3—Tilt the head back until the victim's chin points upward.

4—Push the victim's jaw open until it is jutting out.

5—Put the resuscitator tube into the victim's mouth and pinch his nose shut. If using direct mouth-to-mouth contact, pinch the nostrils shut.

6—Blow into the victim's mouth. Remove your mouth, wait for the victim to return the air, and then repeat.

Adults should receive twelve breaths per minute; children should receive twenty shallow breaths per minute.

SHOCK

A victim of any type of accident can instantly go into shock, and sometimes shock can result in death. Symptoms of shock include gray face, pale lips, blue nails, a fast but weak pulse, a cold sweat, shaking and chills, extreme tiredness, and nausea or vomiting. All of these symptoms may or may not be present in any one individual. It is enough that some of the symptoms exist to assume shock.

Treat shock by keeping the victim warm. Lay him down so that his head is lower than his legs. If you can get the victim to drink, administer hot tea or coffee. Do not force him to drink if he is unconscious. To revive the victim, use smelling salts. In case of a head injury or excessive bleeding, do not give a stimulant of any kind, including tea or coffee. Get him to a doctor as soon as possible. ●

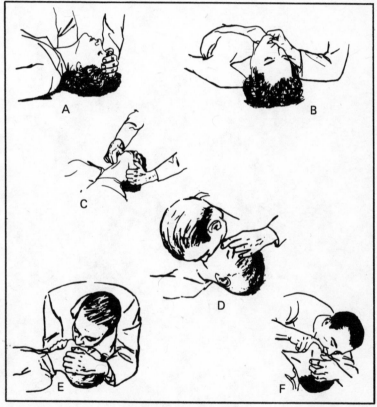

Artificial Respiration

(A) Tilt the person's head back so his chin points upward. (B&C) Pull the jaw into the jutting-out position. (D) Open your mouth wide and place it over the person's mouth while pinching his nostrils, or (E) close his nostrils with your cheek. (F) You can close his mouth and put your mouth over his nose. Blow into the person's mouth or nose.